The
REAL WORLD

Non-fiction and media
11–14

Geoff Barton

Heinemann

Heinemann Educational
Halley Court, Jordan Hill, Oxford OX2 8 EJ
Part of Harcourt Education

Heinemann is the registred trademark of
Harcourt Education Limited

First published 1998

07 06
10 9 8 7

10-digit ISBN 0 435 10118 8
13-digit ISBN 978 0 435101 18 3

Designed and produced by Gecko Ltd, Bicester, Oxon
Cover design by Gecko Ltd, Bicester, Oxon
Illustrations by Paul Davies, Darren Dis – The Art Market, Gecko Ltd (DTP), Rosalind Hudson – Sylvi Poggio Agency, Paul McCaffrey – Sylvi Poggio Agency, Phylis Mahon, Gary Wing.
Printed and bound in Spain by Mateu Cromo

Acknowledgements
The author and publishers would like to thank the following for permission to use copyright material:

Wayland Publishers Ltd for extract from *Know Your Pet* by Anna and Michael Sproule, pp10-11; David Anderson for his children's 'Guide to Museums' in *MAG*, p13; A P Watt Ltd on behalf of Quentin Blake for illustrations, and David Higham Associates on behalf of the Estate of Roald Dahl for extract from *Roald Dahl's Guide to Railway Safety*, pp14-17; Macmillan London for extract from *The Lost World: Junior Novelisation* by Gail Herman (Boxtree, 1977), pp25-27; Universal City Studios Inc and Amblin Entertainment Inc for extracts from *The Lost World: Official Movie Adaptation*, originally published by Topps Comics Inc. Copyright © 1997, pp29-33; Mirror Syndication International for article, 'Boy: I saved my pal from canal' by Stephen White (*The Mirror*, 13 June 1997), p37; Evans Brothers Ltd for extract from *Anne Frank* by Angela Bull (Profile Series 1984), pp38-40; Exley Publications Ltd for extract from *Nelson Mandela* by Benjamin Pogrund (1991), pp41-42; W & R Chambers/Harrap Publishers for extract from *Mythologies* by Fernande Comte (1991), p43; BBC Worldwide Ltd for extract from *Blood and Honey* by Tony Robinson (1993), pp44-45; Tesco Stores Ltd for the leaflet on pp49-52; News International Syndication for article, 'Review of Crunchy Peanut Butter' by Janette Marshall (*The Sunday Times*, 17 June 1990), p55; *Yorkshire Evening Post* for a restaurant review, p56; Compassion in World Farming for the leaflet on p58; *Cambridge Evening News* for news item 'Fen Tiger is secret pigeon fancier' (27 August 1997), p62; *Reader's Digest* for extracts from *Mysteries of the Unexplained* by Richard Marshall, et al (1982), pp63-65; Richard Peyton for 'The Night Flyer of Talyllyn' in *The Ghost Now Standing at Platform One* (Souvenir Press, 1990), pp66-67; Colin Wilson for extract from *The Book of Great Mysteries* (Robinson Publishing, 1986), pp68-69; Reed Consumer Books Ltd for extract from *The Beaver Book of Horror* by Daniel Farson (Hamlyn, 1979), pp70-72; William Cook for extract from *Ha Bloody Ha* (Fourth Estate, 1994), pp74-75; BBC Television for its informational notes 'So you want to write comedy for BBC Television?', p76; David Wilkinson Associates on behalf of John Cleese and Connie Booth for extract from *The Complete Fawlty Towers* (Methuen, 1988), pp78-80; Macmillan London for extracts from *Bean: The Script Book* by Atkinson, Driscoll and Curtis (Boxtree, 1997), pp81-85; Ewan MacNaughton Associates on behalf of Telegraph Group Ltd for the review by Alistair Fraser (*The Sunday Telegraph*, 6 July 1997), p86; News International Syndication for the review by Tom Shone (*The Sunday Times*, 10 August 1997), p86; Health Education Authority for the leaflet on pp90-91; The Donkey Sanctuary for the advert on p94; ACTIONAID for the advert on p95; Roger Pett for extracts and notes on writing commercials, pp96-99; Ladybird Books Ltd for extracts from *Exploring Space* by Roy Worvill, pp103-104; The Independent Newspaper Publishing for news item from *The Independent On-Line* (1 August 1997), pp108-109; HarperCollins Publishers, Australia for 'Killing a Kookaburra' from 'Kill to Eat' in *Stradbroke Dreamtime* by Oodgeroo Noonuccal, pp115-117; Penguin Books Ltd for 'At home in Egypt' from *Oleander Jacaranda: A Childhood Perceived* by Penelope Lively. Copyright © Penelope Lively, 1994 (Viking, 1994), pp118-120; Macmillan London for 'Dealing with a truant' from *A Century of Childhood* by Stephen Humphries, Joanna Mack, Robert Perks (Sidgwick and Jackson, 1988), pp121-122; Jean Hawkes for extract from translation of *The London Journal of Flora Tristan* (Virago, 1982), p124-125; News International Syndication for 'A Life in the day of Guy the Gorilla' by Hunter Davies (*The Sunday Times*, 4 December 1977), p127.

The publishers have made every effort to trace the copyright holders, but if they have inadvertently overlooked any, they will be pleased to make the necessary arrangements at the first opportunity.

The publishers would also like to thank the following for permission to reproduce photographs on the pages noted:

Trevor Hill, p10; London Transport Museum, p13; Moviestore, pp26, 81; Ross Parry, p37; Corbis, p38; AKG, p39; Mayibuye Centre, p41; Hadden Davies, p54; Fox/Humane Society USA, p58; Comedy Store, p74; Off the Kerb Productions, p74; Express Newspapers, p75; BBC, pp77, 78, 79; Polygram, pp83, 84; Karen Fuchs, p86; The Donkey Sanctuary, p94; ACTIONAID, p95; J Allan Cash, pp96, 97; Direct Holidays, pp96, 97; Kobal Collection, p111; Popperfoto, p121; David Reed/Sunday Times, p127.

Contents

WESTON
COLLEGE
LIBRARY

Introduction

The Real World is a collection of non-fiction and media texts for KS3 English. It includes a wide range of different forms and genres, such as:

- leaflets
- letters
- instruction sheets
- interviews
- newspaper articles
- graphic novels
- advertisements
- biographies
- magazine articles
- film scripts
- radio commercial scripts
- … and more.

Texts like these are invaluable in the classroom. They can prompt lively discussion, good quality analytical work, and develop students' awareness of style and genre. In the frenzy of classroom life, however, they can also be hard to track down and the danger is that we resort to another dusty pairing of contrasting newspaper articles.

The main aim of this collection is to give you support by providing a lively mix of texts which you probably wouldn't otherwise have to hand.

Organisation

The texts are grouped thematically. Each unit has its **starting points** – a brisk, active introduction to the theme. This is followed by the first **text**, with **word banks**, where necessary, to help to clarify certain words.

Each text is followed by a small number of **activities**. These vary in style. Some use drama or role-play. Others test comprehension. Some expect analysis or rewriting of the text. Together, they are designed to strengthen students' awareness of the content and language of the writer's work.

At the end of each unit there is a group of two or three **assignments**. These are broader, more open-ended tasks which are designed to lead to lively, interesting responses. The emphasis in these is largely upon independent written class– and homework.

The Real World is structured sequentially, with the more accessible units early in the book, and the more demanding units later. The nine units can be used flexibly: they might, for example, be divided into three units each for Years 7, 8 and 9, to match departmental planning for schemes of work.

But I leave the use of the book to you. It was great fun to unearth such a range of texts. I hope you will enjoy using them in the classroom, and that the activities help your students to develop a familiarity with a greater range of media and non-fiction genres.

Geoff Barton

How to ...

Starting points

How good are you at giving clear instructions? Can you: Get the order right? Keep the language plain and simple? Give enough but not too much detail?

Have a go … Imagine that someone has asked you how to get from your English classroom to the school reception. Try to give clear step-by-step instructions, either verbal or written. If you give your instructions aloud, try not to use your hands at all. Make the words do all the work.

Work in pairs on this. Read or listen to each other's instructions, and give each other advice on how your instructions could have been clearer.

Now look at the different examples of instructions throughout this unit …

Now that's magic

The instructions which follow are from *The Little Book of Magic Tricks*. We all love to amaze our friends with a bit of conjuring, so try this trick. As you read the instructions, notice how they have been written and organised. Then prepare to astonish your family, with the 'Penny through the elbow trick'.

PENNY THROUGH THE ELBOW

The penny is at your elbow, but the audience will be in the palm of your hand

the
EFFECT:
An ordinary penny disappears into your elbow.

what
YOU'LL NEED:
A penny
This trick is performed while seated at a table.

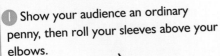 Show your audience an ordinary penny, then roll your sleeves above your elbows.

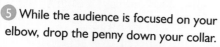 Hold the penny in your left hand, and start rubbing it against your right elbow. The fingers of your left hand should

completely cover the penny. Tell the audience that you are going to rub the penny right into your arm.

 'Accidentally' let the penny slip from behind your fingers and onto the table. Apologize to the audience while you pick up the penny with your *right* hand and pass it to your left hand. Repeat step 2.

4 Once again drop the penny. Pick it up with your right hand, but this time *pretend* to pass it to your left hand. Continue rubbing your elbow with your left hand, as if the penny were still in that hand.

5 While the audience is focused on your elbow, drop the penny down your collar.

6 As you continue to rub, lift one finger at a time from your elbow, until it is clear that the penny has vanished.

Steven Zorn, *The Little Book of Magic Tricks*

Activities

1 On a scale of 1 to 5, decide how clear you thought the magic trick instructions were.

Not very good   **Very good**
1 ← 2 — 3 — 4 → 5

Look back at the instructions and ask yourself these questions:

- Were the instructions in the right order?
- Was any essential information missed out?
- Was the language easy to follow?
- Were the illustrations helpful?

Compare your response with a friend's. Discuss how you might have improved the instructions.

2 Create your own instruction sheet. Choose one of the following topics or a different one agreed with your teacher:

- How to do a magic trick you know.
- How to make a telephone call from a public phone box.
- How to clean your teeth.
- How to install a computer game.

Hints

- Think about who you are writing the sheet for – readers of your own age, younger or older readers?
- Remember to keep the language clear – use short sentences and familiar words.
- Tell the reader in advance any important information, such as items of equipment they will need before they start.
- Use simple illustrations if these will help the reader to follow your ideas.
- Number your instructions, so that the reader is always clear about the order.

Ask a friend to read your instructions. Can s/he follow them? Discuss anything you could have improved.

Finally, write a paragraph about how you tackled your instruction sheet. You should include the problems you met, how you overcame them, which parts of the sheet worked best, how you might have done it differently, and so on.

Your pet rat

People have mixed feelings about rats. Some people are terrified even at the thought of them. Others admire their intelligence and keep them as pets. The extracts which follow are taken from an information book which gives advice about the health care of rats and mice.

Health care

Rats and mice are healthy animals. Most rats will live for three years, and mice for two, with few health problems. But you must give them a good diet, clean their cages regularly and keep them away from damp and draughts.

Signs of ill-health

You should always watch for any signs of ill-health in your pets. They should breathe easily without wheezing or snuffles, and their droppings should be firm and not runny. There should be no discharge from the eyes or nose. They should eat well and take an interest in you when you talk to them or hold out your hand. An animal that has an untidy-looking coat, or that sits hunched up, is likely to be ill. If so, **isolate** it in another cage on its own.

▼ This girl is treating an injured Black Rex rat. Antiseptic creams can be obtained from a vet. Any wound should be cleaned with a cotton bud and the cream applied with another clean cotton bud.

Illness and treatment

Breathing troubles are sometimes caused by dust in the hay or litter. A change in the kind of litter and bedding you are using may cure the problem.

Loose droppings, with stains under the tail, can be caused by feeding too much greenstuff or fruit. Feed only mash for a day or two until the droppings look normal again.

Overgrown front teeth are sometimes a problem. Rats and mice usually keep their teeth in trim by gnawing. If they do not gnaw enough the incisors grow too long for the animal to be able to eat properly. Then it may be necessary for you to take the animal to a vet who can trim the incisors painlessly.

All animals need a chemical called **vitamin C** to keep the skin and hair in good condition. A balanced diet should give rats and mice all the vitamin C they need, but bald patches on the coat, or sores on the skin, are a sign that they are not getting enough. The pet shop can supply vitamin C tablets which you can dissolve in the drinking water or mix with food.

If your pets have parasites in their coats, a dusting powder can be bought from a pet shop.

Anna and Michael
Sproule, *Know Your Pet*

Activities

1 Read these statements based on the information in the extracts. For each statement, decide whether it is true (T) or false (F). If you think there is not enough information to know the answer, write (N).

1 Rats can suffer breathing problems.
2 Healthy rats have long, sharp teeth.
3 You shouldn't feed rats too much fruit.
4 If a rat has bald patches in its fur, it is getting too much vitamin C.
5 Rats like gnawing wood.
6 The life-expectancy of a rat is two years.
7 A sign of illness is when a rat sits hunched up.
8 You should always keep rats in cages on their own.
9 Rats are easy pets to look after.
10 Rats are friendly.

2 Based on the information in 'Your pet rat', create a page of 'dos and don'ts' giving readers instant guidance on how to care for their rat. Use the example below to help you.

Looking after your pet rat: Some dos and don'ts

Do	Don't
check the length of your rat's teeth regularly	leave it without something to gnaw on

The Real World

Museums, galleries and kids

The article on page 13 is taken from a magazine called *MAG – Museums and Galleries*. It is aimed at young people and gives them advice on how to take their parents around museums. Notice how it pokes fun at the way adults sometimes talk about children.

Activities

1 What picture of adults does the article give? Look at the list of statements below and decide which one best sums up the way adults are presented. Then try to find an example from the article to support your opinion.

- Adults are idiots.
- Adults need a lot of attention.
- Adults cannot really think for themselves.
- Adults will learn a great deal if they are encouraged in the right way.

2 Which of the ten tips do you think is the most useful? Which do you disagree with?

3 Imagine you took an adult with you around a place that you know – for example, your school or a favourite shop. Write an account of your visit. You might mention:

- how the adult reacted to what s/he saw
- how s/he behaved during the visit
- the kinds of questions the adult asked you
- any activities the adult joined in.

To make your account funny and entertaining, write about the adult as if s/he were a child. You could start like this:

> I followed the advice of David Anderson's guide and took my dad to Bond's department store in Norwich. He was quite well behaved, though he threw a bit of a tantrum as I got him dressed to go out. On the way to the shop he asked some very silly questions ...

A unique pull-out-and-keep guide for adults and kids on how to get the most out of visiting museums and galleries. Brought to you by *MAG*, the magazine of London's museums and galleries.

MUSEUMS, GALLERIES AND KIDS
A HOW-TO-DO-IT GUIDE

How to Take Your Adults Around Museums

David Anderson, head of education at the V&A, offers his ten top tips ...

So, you've decided to take your adults to a museum? Well they have earned a day out – but just look at the poor creatures! Tired and stressed, they may just be tempted to collapse in a heap and grope for the remote control button on the television. So, use your undoubted skills of persuasion to convince them that what you enjoy is exactly what they want as well.

As you probably realise, this could be tricky. Adults often don't like to count how long it is since they were your age, and may have forgotten how to enjoy, rather than just shuffle around, a museum. Be gentle with them, but firm. Here are my ten tips on taking your adults round museums:

1 Remember their creature comforts. Adults are (almost) human and need lots of time to enjoy cups of tea, visit the toilet, buy postcards and generally relax. Fortunately, so do you.

Look here mum... Encourage your adults to talk about what they see

2 Encourage them to really see some of the wonderful things that are in the museum – taking just a little more time to learn how to explore with their eyes. Museums are different to books or television.

3 Persuade them also to experience what they see. Museums can educate the heart as well as the mind and are about feelings as much as facts.

4 Get them talking about what they see and experience. Talking helps them understand and remember, and you know what their memory can be like!

5 Like you, adults need questions and stories to maintain their interest. Encourage them to ask questions as well.

6 Find some things they like, and some you like, and make sure they spend time on each. Be patient if what they want to find out about is different from what attracts you.

7 Persuade them to use their imagination. Luckily you have lots of it and can help them out a good deal in this department.

8 If there is a chance to take part or to join in an activity, then please encourage them to take it. Remember, adults are just as likely to enjoy being active as you, but they can sometimes be a little shy.

9 Tell the museum what you think about their provision for families. Be very honest – a good museum will want to know what you think so that they can improve their service.

10 If you like the museum, please visit it again. Adults can only manage a little before they get what doctors call 'museum fatigue'. Little and often is better than too much and never again.

David Anderson is head of education at the Victoria and Albert Museum and the author of 'A Common Wealth – Museums and Learning in the UK', available free from the Department of National Heritage Public Enquiry Point by calling 0171 211 6200.

Roald Dahl's Guide to Railway Safety

In the 1980s Roald Dahl was asked to support a campaign to make railways safer for children by writing a booklet called *Roald Dahl's Guide to Railway Safety*. Before the advice on safety begins, Roald Dahl writes an introduction about the difference between adults and children.

I have a **VERY DIFFICULT** job here.

Young people are fed up with being told by grown-ups **WHAT TO DO** and **WHAT NOT TO DO**.

They get that all through their young lives. And now I am going to have to tell you **WHAT TO DO** and **WHAT NOT TO DO**, but this time it's a bit different because the **DOs** and **DON'Ts** that I am going to give you may easily **SAVE YOUR LIFE**.

That is the only reason I agreed to write this message to you.

But before I start with the heavy stuff, I'd like to tell you my own theory about grown-ups and their **DOs** and **DON'Ts** and why a lot of them are not very good at dealing with children.

I am totally convinced that most grown-ups have completely forgotten what it was like to be a child between say the age of five and ten. They all **think** they can remember. Parents think they can remember and so do teachers. Some of course actually can, but very few. It is after all quite difficult to remember exactly what it felt like to be a small person when you yourself haven't been one for thirty or forty years. That's a long time ago.

I can remember exactly what it was like. I am certain I can. If I couldn't then I would not be able to write my sort of books for children. Let me tell you how I see this whole difficult question because I think it is interesting.

When you are young, you have not finished growing. You are therefore physically shorter, usually by two feet or more, than the grown-ups around you. This is the first thing the grown-ups have forgotten. If a grown-up really wants to find out what it is like to live in a young person's world, let him or her get down on hands and knees and go about like that for a week. The first thing they will then discover is that all the other grown-ups in the room tower above them and they actually have to crane their necks to look at their faces. It is always like that with a small child. the child is surrounded by GIANTS, and the trouble with these beastly GIANTS is that they seem to spend most of their lives telling the child WHAT TO DO and WHAT NOT TO DO.

What the child does not understand is that unfortunately the GIANTS **have** to do this. It is the only way to bring up a child properly. When you are born you are an uncivilised little savage with bad habits and no manners and it is the job of the GIANTS (your parents and your teachers) to train you and discipline you. The child hates this and resists it fiercely. Yet it has to be done. It is all part of the process of turning the uncivilised and savage little child into a good citizen.

"Say please…say thank you… go and wash your hands…take your elbows off the table…don't spit…don't come in here with muddy shoes…turn off the telly and do your homework…" The stream of orders is endless.

What is the result of all this? I'll tell you precisely what it is. Deep down inside the child's mind (subconsciously), the giants become THE ENEMY. Your teachers become THE ENEMY. Even your loving parents become THE ENEMY.

Not outwardly but inwardly, subconsciously.

This explains very clearly why **Matilda** is far and away the most popular children's book I have written and was bought by over half a million children in Britain alone in the first six months. In it there are a pair of perfectly revolting parents and a foul tyrant of a teacher.

The young reader is invited to hate them all and he does. He says to himself, "Thank goodness we have here a writer who understands our secret feelings." Children may not realise it themselves, but that is the real reason why **Matilda** is so popular among them.

But enough of that. Having made my excuses, I must now regretfully become one of those unpopular giants who tells you WHAT TO DO and WHAT NOT TO DO. This is something I have never done in any of my books. I have been careful never to preach, never to be moralistic and never to convey any message to the reader. I hate doing it so much that I think I will find just one more excuse to put off the preaching. So, I am going to spend another two minutes telling you why I have always loved trains and railways.

Sixty-four years ago, when I was a small boy of eight, there were very few cars on the roads and we went everywhere by train. There were precious few lorries about either. Nearly all goods traffic went by train. Our roads were clean and uncrowded, and in our cities the air was not polluted with gases from a million exhaust-pipes. It was a lovely world to live in, but the motor-car has ruined it. It has also, to some extent, ruined **us**. Instead of walking to school as we always used to do in the olden days, even if it was a three mile journey, nearly every child of today gets taken there in a car. Everyone goes everywhere by car these days, and perhaps in a few hundred years from now our great-great-great grandchildren will be born with hardly any legs at all because they won't have any use for them.

moralistic – telling someone the difference between right and wrong

The flood of motor-cars and lorries and trucks onto our roads in recent years is a tragedy for nature and for the environment and for our health. We never missed them when I was young and we all loved our train journeys.

Oh, how we loved those trains in the good old days! We used to stand for hours beside the railway line or leaning over a bridge waiting for the next one to come rushing past, and we would write down the numbers of the engines and also their names. (King George V, Dunraven Castle). All the big ones had names. We also collected pictures of them on cigarette-cards. Nowadays children worship motor-cars instead, horrible noisy machines made of steel that kill hundreds of thousands of people every year. Give me the train any day. And I hope that in the end our roads will become so clogged with all these fume-belching cars and lorries that everyone will give them up and start going by the train once again. I, and indeed a lot of other people, feel that this is going to happen sooner than you think, and that many of you will be happily using the train in the near future, especially for longer journeys.

Activities

1 Roald Dahl has a number of theories about children and adults. Do you agree with him?

- He believes adults have forgotten what it was like to be a child because it is so long since they were one themselves.

- He says adults spend so long telling children how to behave that children learn to see adults as the 'enemy'.

- He also says that *Matilda* was his most popular children's book because it contains the secret feelings of children – that all adults are hateful.

2 In the final section of his introduction, Roald Dahl writes about his memories of trains. He hopes that one day people will use trains again instead of relying so much on cars. Look at the negative words he uses to describe cars:

horrible   noisy   clogged   fume-belching

Imagine you are writing an introduction like this in a hundred years' time, and you look back to a golden age of motor cars. Imagine that cars seem a really attractive and relaxing way of travelling. Write a couple of paragraphs looking back at the joys of the motor car. You might start like this:

Oh, how we loved those cars in the good old days! We would all eagerly pile in, smelling the polish and wax where it had just been cleaned. The engine would roar into life ...

ASSIGNMENTS

1 Demonstrations

Working with a partner, put together a four to six minute demonstration of how to do or make something.
You might demonstrate:

- how to mend a puncture

- how to do origami (paper-folding)

- how to perform a magic trick

- how to make a pencil holder out of an old washing-up bottle.

First decide what you will demonstrate. Work out the different steps you will need to show. Decide:

- how you will share the roles in the demonstration

- how you will introduce it

- what you will say

- whether you need any visual aids (whiteboard, OHP, etc).

  Now rehearse your demonstration and then perform it to the rest of the group.

2 Pet Advice sheet

Think of an animal you know something about, perhaps one you have kept as a pet. Choose a topic (such as, feeding, health care, exercising, grooming or cleaning) and create a one-page advice sheet for new owners of this kind of pet. Try to:

- use clear, straightforward language to give the reader advice

- keep paragraphs short

- use bullet points if they will help to present information clearly

- include illustrations to add visual interest and to help explain your points

- if you use a computer, use different fonts in a variety of sizes, underlining, bold and boxes to make your advice sheet clear.

ASSIGNMENTS

3 Places to go

1 Imagine someone of your own age has just moved to your area and is looking for places to visit and things to do. Make a list of the places you would recommend and what you would say about each one.

2 Put together a page for a guide book for children of your own age, suggesting different places to visit. Include as much information as you can, set out clearly. Look at the example below to give you ideas:

Name of
place to visit

Places to visit in Suffolk

Rollerbury, Bury St Edmunds ●

This is a good place to go with your friends rather than your parents. It is a huge skating rink, with plenty of other activities on site too.

Open most days. £3 admission. ●

Details

Description

4 Advice leaflet for children

Look back at Roald Dahl's advice on railway safety (pages 14–17). Put together your own leaflet aimed at children aged between eight and twelve. Choose either of the topics below:

- safe cycling in the dark - hints on how to be seen
- playing safely - places you should not play (for example, building sites, near railway lines and busy roads).

Make your leaflet one side of A4 paper. Remember your target audience and try to:

- keep your language simple and direct
- keep the style informal
- use questions and bullet points to add variety
- use illustrations to add interest.

Creatures of terror

Starting points

Human beings have mixed feelings about animals. We love to keep pets, and yet we happily hunt some creatures for food, or just for pleasure. We put pictures of fluffy kittens on posters and chocolate-box advertising, and use hyenas and wolves to suggest criminals, crooks and liars.

Our record on caring for pets in Britain is amongst the worst in Europe. Year after year animals are hurt, abandoned, and cruelly abused.

Yet animals fascinate us – even those which fill us with terror: scorpions, giant spiders, dinosaurs and snakes …

Which creature are you most likely to have nightmares about? Do you have any animal phobias – really deep fears of creatures like spiders or snakes? Which animals fill you with terror?

Deadly serious

Sometimes terrifying creatures can be closer than you think. Look at this news story reported on ITN's website ...

phobia – powerful fear of something
cardiovascular – related to the heart and blood-vessels
complacent – calm
lethal – deadly
masquerade – disguised as something else

DEADLY SCORPIONS MASQUERADE AS HARMLESS PETS

Lethal scorpions could be lurking in homes after being mistakenly sold as harmless pets.

The Royal Society for the Prevention of Cruelty to Animals has warned that pet shops in the London area have been selling deadly scorpions from the Buthid family for £2.99, believing them to be non-poisonous.

In fact the Buthid – normally found in India, Africa and the Middle East – is so venomous that it can kill a human within 30 minutes.

The venom attacks the human's nervous system, causing cardiovascular complications which eventually result in death.

Experts are warning people who have bought scorpions not to be complacent just because the animals are tiny.

An RSPCA spokesperson said: 'These are nasty little creatures. As juveniles they are not lethal but when they are two years old or more they are very lethal.'

Around 12 Buthids are believed to be masquerading as people's pets.

Activities

1 Check your understanding of the text on deadly scorpions.

1 Where are the scorpions being sold?

2 How much do they cost?

3 What are these deadly scorpions called?

4 Where do they normally live?

5 How do they kill people?

6 Why could people who have bought them be deceived into thinking they are harmless creatures?

7 Are the creatures deadly all their lives?

2 Work in pairs or in small groups. Make up a role-play based on these events:

- you see scorpions being sold cheaply in a pet shop

- as a joke, you buy one for a friend

- you take it home and present it to your friend. What is her/his reaction?

- in the background the television is on. Suddenly the story of the Buthid scorpions comes on. What happens ...?

In a group of four take the following roles:

- pet shop assistant
- friend
- buyer
- newsreader.

Start by working out your roles. Brainstorm how the role-play should begin. Then plan your role-play to create a piece of drama which lasts three to four minutes.

As a follow-up role-play, imagine you take the scorpion back to the pet shop to say what you have seen on television and demand your money back.

- What will happen if the pet shop owner refuses ...?

Dinosaur facts

Ever since the first discovery of dinosaur fossils, almost two hundred years ago, humans have been fascinated by these huge and terrifying creatures. We even like to imagine that a relative of those early monsters might still be swimming around a loch in Scotland.

The following extracts try to give us the facts about dinosaurs and answer some of our questions about what these remarkable creatures must have been like.

How successful are the extracts in informing us about dinosaurs?

What colour were dinosaurs?

Nobody knows for certain what colour dinosaurs were. But it is probable that, like most reptiles, they had dull brownish or greenish skins. Their colouring would have helped to camouflage them, or to frighten away enemies. Many animals of today have colouring that serves these purposes. Only in a few cases has dinosaur skin been preserved as a fossil. Even when it has been found, the pigment cells have seldom been in existence.

Do we know what they ate?

It has been relatively easy to discover which of the dinosaurs were meat eaters and which were plant eaters. The meat eaters had well-developed – often very powerful – jaws, and had sharp teeth with which to tear flesh from their prey and chew it. Also, they were built as hunters. Either they were very speedy – and, as a result, could catch their prey easily – or they were extremely strong and were armed with vicious claws and talons. The plant eaters usually had teeth adapted to grinding their food. In some cases, it is clear that a particular dinosaur was a plant eater because the front of its jaw projected in a horny beak. This would have been useless for eating meat, but would have been very helpful in reaching and cutting tough vegetation.

Which were the last dinosaurs?

The end of an era. Towards the end of the Cretaceous period, the long reign of the dinosaur came to an end. No dinosaur fossils have been found in any rocks deposited after the end of the period. Dinosaurs had been the lords of the Earth for some 150 million years. They had evolved a great variety of forms and had managed to live in almost every kind of environment.

Who ruled the world after the dinosaurs?

For a long time, the mammals had been overshadowed by the great reptiles. Now they took over the world. They included animals as varied as the dull creodont, the timid eohippus, the ferocious sabre-toothed cat – and Man and the creatures of his world.

Which was the first dinosaur named?

The first dinosaur named was the large, flesh-eating *Megalosaurus*, which lived in Jurassic times. Though it was not identified until 1824, it had been known for a long time. A bone of a creature that may have been *Megalosaurus* was pictured in a book published in the 1600s. At that time, people thought that it was the remains of a gigantic man.

Megalosaurus

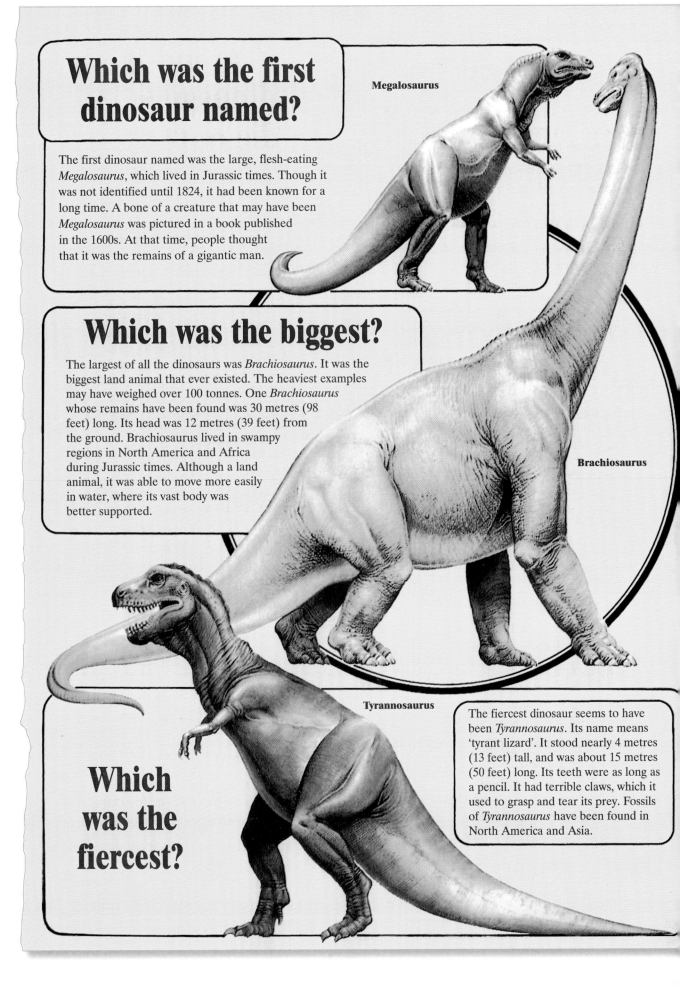

Which was the biggest?

The largest of all the dinosaurs was *Brachiosaurus*. It was the biggest land animal that ever existed. The heaviest examples may have weighed over 100 tonnes. One *Brachiosaurus* whose remains have been found was 30 metres (98 feet) long. Its head was 12 metres (39 feet) from the ground. Brachiosaurus lived in swampy regions in North America and Africa during Jurassic times. Although a land animal, it was able to move more easily in water, where its vast body was better supported.

Brachiosaurus

Tyrannosaurus

Which was the fiercest?

The fiercest dinosaur seems to have been *Tyrannosaurus*. Its name means 'tyrant lizard'. It stood nearly 4 metres (13 feet) tall, and was about 15 metres (50 feet) long. Its teeth were as long as a pencil. It had terrible claws, which it used to grasp and tear its prey. Fossils of *Tyrannosaurus* have been found in North America and Asia.

Have many other kinds of animals become extinct?

During the Earth's long history, thousands of different kinds of creatures have evolved, have flourished for long or short periods and have then died out. One of the most recent to become extinct was the bird called the *dodo*. The last dodo died in 1681. We know what dodos looked like because they were painted by a Flemish artist.

Why did the dinosaurs die out?

The dinosaurs probably died out because the Earth's landscape, climate and vegetation had changed. Their bodies and habits could not adapt fast enough to enable them to live in the new conditions. Possibly, they were not able to find the sort of food they needed. As many parts of the world became cooler, they may have been unable to withstand the cold. They may also have been harmed by winds and drought, or even by radiation from Space.

Anthony Harvey, *The Unreal World of the Dinosaurs*

Activities

1 Now check your understanding of the extracts. Which word or phrase fills each gap in this paragraph? The first gaps need one word each; later gaps need several words.

The first named dinosaur ate ¹_____. The last Dodo died in ²____. The biggest dinosaur discovered grew up to ³_____ metres in length. It lived in ⁴_____ and ⁵_____ _____. It lived on ⁶_____ but was able to move more easily in ⁷_____. The fiercest dinosaur was called ⁸_____. We can tell that they were fierce because ⁹_____. We are not sure what colour dinosaurs were because ¹⁰_____. We imagine that they were ¹¹_____ or ¹²_____. We can tell whether a dinosaur is a plant- or meat-eater by ¹³_____. Dinosaurs probably died out because:
¹⁴_____
_____
_____

2 The text contains some information that is not definite, so the writer uses words like 'probably' and 'may'. There are some facts in the text too. Find five pieces of information which seem to be definite facts.

3 Use a library, reference books or CD-ROM to find information on one of these topics:
- the Jurassic period
- stegosaurus
- diplodocus
- dodo
- brachiosaurus.

Either: make a two-minute factual presentation to the rest of the class, telling them what you have found out.

Or: write a 150-word factual account of your chosen topic, *using your own words*. Make the style of your writing clear so that someone of your own age can easily understand it. Include an illustration if that helps.

The Lost World: novelisation

Following the huge success of *Jurassic Park*, film-maker Steven Spielberg made *The Lost World*. Like many major Hollywood movies, it was also used to market products such as books and toys.

The extract which follows is taken from the 'junior novelisation'. This means that the storyline of the film has been rewritten as a novel for a younger audience, probably nine to thirteen-year-olds.

The story so far …

Nick, Eddie and Ian are tracking down their colleague, Sarah, who has disappeared in the jungle. They use a satellite phone to track the red *X* which shows where she is …

The three men started down a jungle trail. Trees and vines blocked out most of the sun. Ian checked their hand-held monitor. Little by little, the *X* was drawing closer to the triangle. Ian started to walk faster.

Finally they stepped out of the bush. They stood in a dry river-bed.

5 Ian glanced at the screen. The *X* was right on top of the triangle.

And Sarah was nowhere to be seen.

Ian's eyes swept over the sand and dirt and trees. 'Sarah should be here!' he cried.

'Over there!' Nick pointed. He pointed to a battered backpack on the
10 ground. He picked it up.

'Oh, no,' Eddie exclaimed. The pack was beaten up and smeared with dirt.

Ian tore it open and pulled out Sarah's satellite phone.

'She must be nearby,' Nick said, picking the backpack up and sling-
15 ing it over his shoulder.

'We'll split up. We'll cover more ground.'

'Absolutely not!' said Ian. 'We stay together. Predators look for strays that have split off from their group.'

'But –' Nick began to protest. Then suddenly he wheeled around. Did
20 those trees just move? Sway? No, he decided. It was nothing. Maybe the wind.

'I'll take the far edge,' he continued. 'Eddie you –'

Creak! Swish! Nick stopped. That was no wind. The trees were definitely moving. Something was there.

25 Ian signalled them to keep quiet. Eddie readied his gun. Nick turned on his video camera.

predators – animals which hunt other animals

Then something large and greenish-grey brushed by the trees right beside them. The three men jumped.

'What was it?' Ian whispered.

30 'Something big,' Eddie hissed back.

'How big?'

'Big enough to worry about!'

Above the trees, they saw a row of plates glide by – some kind of bony armour. Nick gasped as he peered through the bush. It was a

35 Stegosaurus!

The mighty dinosaur whipped its spiky tail back and forth as it crashed through the jungle.

A second stegosaur, about half the size of the first, lumbered behind it. A juvenile! And behind the two, came the biggest stegosaur of all.

40 It was a stegosaur family! Eddie couldn't help it. He burst into laughter as the animals plodded past. In a flash, Ian clapped a hand over Eddie's mouth. Then he lifted a thick blanket of leaves. There, in a large clearing, stood an entire herd of stegosaurs. All ages. All sizes.

Quickly Nick set up his equipment. Ian scanned the clearing. Still no

45 sign of Sarah. But wait! He saw a figure, crouched behind some rocks. Yes, it was Sarah – dressed in field gear, scribbling furiously on a notepad. She turned to watch the stegosaur family, caught sight of the research team, and waved.

'She's gutsy,' Nick whispered.

50 'She's nuts,' Ian hissed.

Grinning, Sarah hurried over. 'Ian!' she said breathlessly. 'I'm so happy you're here!'

Then she turned back to the animals. 'Can you believe this? A family group! Babies staying with their parents! I've seen nests. Eggs –'

55 Ian grabbed her arm, interrupting. 'Are you all right? Were you attacked?'

'What do you mean?' Sarah said.

Ian held up the backpack.

'Oh, that's how it always looks,' she told him. 'It's my lucky pack.'

60 She spotted one of Nick's cameras. 'Hey, you don't mind if I borrow this, do you? I dropped mine in the water yesterday.'

She took the camera and scrambled back into the clearing. She crept along beside the baby stegosaur, snapping shot after shot.

Nick grinned at Ian. 'Should we rescue her now?' he joked. 'Or after
65 lunch?'

Whirr! Just then, the roll of film ended and the camera suddenly rewound. Startled, the stegosaurs jumped. The biggest one swung toward Sarah. Its plates bristled like a cat's fur standing on end.

Silently, Sarah began to move away.

70 'Sarah!' Ian shouted.

The dinosaur spun instantly toward him. Its tail whipped through the air. *Whizz!* Straight for Sarah. She leaped back, and the tail missed her by inches.

Then the animal twisted its head toward Sarah. It raised its tail, ready
75 to strike again.

Sarah crawled like a shot into a hollow log. Safe, she thought.

Crunch! Spikes drilled through her cover, as the creature's tail slammed down on the rotting wood. Sharp bone grazed Sarah's face.

As the dinosaur struggled to free its tail, Sarah quickly crawled out of
80 the log. But by then the animal had lost interest. As soon as he was free, he followed the rest of the herd into the jungle. In seconds, they disappeared.

Ian, Eddie, and Nick rushed to Sarah.

'Isn't it great?' she cried.

85 Ian shook his head and frowned.

Gail Herman, *The Lost World: Junior Novelisation*

stegosaurus – dinosaur with spikes along its spine

Activities

1 In the novelisation Nick thinks Sarah is 'gutsy'. Ian says she is 'nuts'. Based on your reading of the text, what do you think?

2 At the end of the extract, 'Ian shook his head and frowned'. Why do you think this is?

3 Sarah has gone into the jungle to watch dinosaurs. Crouched behind rocks, she scribbles furiously on a notepad. Look again at the description of what she sees.

Imagine what she is writing on her notepad, and write her notes. You might start like this:

> I can't believe what's in front of my eyes ...

4 Use a storyboard like the one below to show the story of this written extract in frames (pictures). Just do a quick sketch, labelling any parts that are not clear. What words would you put into each box?

You should use six to twelve frames.

The Lost World: graphic novel

Graphic novels are adult comics. They tell stories through pictures and are often based on science fiction or crime stories. The following extract, from the graphic novel version of *The Lost World*, tells the same story as the novelisation extract on pages 25–27. What differences do you notice?

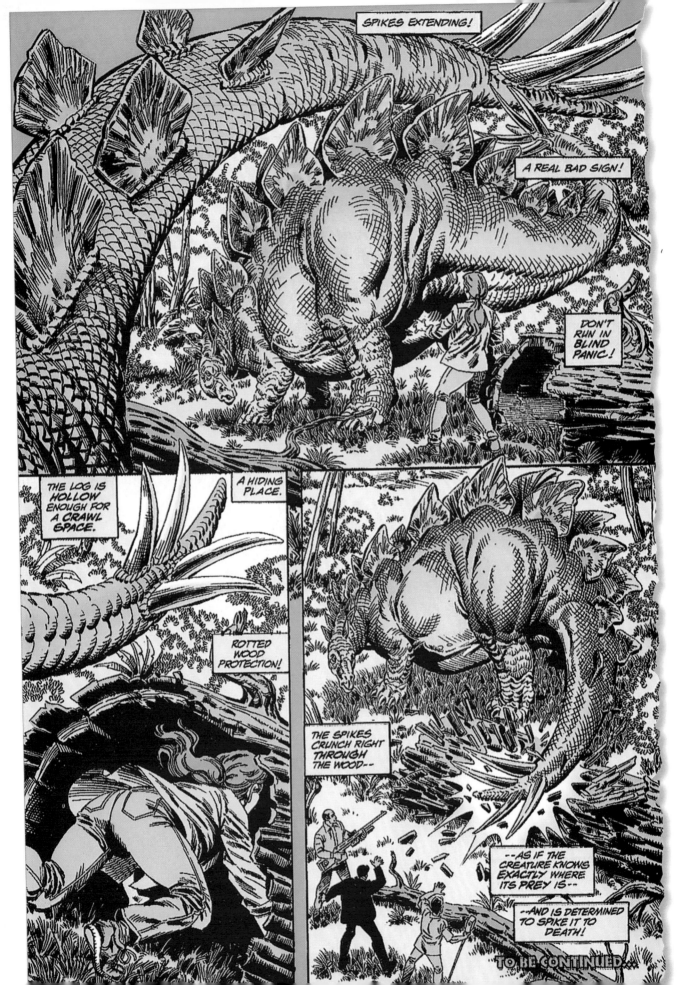

Don McGregor, Jeff Butler, Claude St Aubin,
The Lost World: Official movie adaptation

Activities

1 Use a table like the one below to compare the similarities and differences between the version of the story in the graphic novel and the version in the novelisation on pages 25–27. Think about:

- the storyline itself – parts that are left in and parts that are cut
- the characters of the men
- the character of Sarah
- what the characters say
- the atmosphere of the jungle
- the speed of the action in each version of the story.

Similarities	Differences

2 Based on your comparison, which of these statements do you agree with?
In the novelisation:

- there is more description of the scene
- we learn more about Sarah's feelings
- it is easier to imagine exactly what is going on
- there is less detail.

In the graphic novel:

- Sarah seems more strong-minded
- the storyline is more confusing
- the dinosaurs are more terrifying
- the story moves more slowly
- some of the language sounds a bit corny.

Discuss your opinions in pairs or in small groups. Support your viewpoint with an example from either text.

ASSIGNMENTS

1 Pets

Some people see pets in a really positive way. Pets provide companionship and affection, and, because you have to look after them, they make you feel responsible for something. People who haven't time for real pets can even buy electronic ones.

Other people think this is crazy. They think pets are a sign of weakness. If you need to own a pet, it's because you need to pretend to have power by controlling something. If you have a very unusual pet, it's because you want to attract attention to yourself. What do you think?

Write a paragraph about your attitude to pets – positive or negative. Then write four paragraphs about a pet you have owned or would like to own, answering these questions, each in a separate paragraph:

1 Why did/do you want a pet?

2 Why that pet in particular?

3 Describe the routines you followed or would follow to look after your pet.

4 If you have already owned a pet, what did you enjoy or dislike about owning her/him?

2 Presenting facts

The information text about dinosaurs on pages 22 – 24 shows how you can take a complicated subject and present it clearly and quite simply.

Choose your own topic (it doesn't have to be anything to do with creatures), for example:

● a figure in history who interests you

● the way a machine, such as a computer, works.

Create a double page spread about your topic for an information book. It needs to be as clear and easy-to-follow as you can make it.

Work out a draft version first, and remember to use:

● pictures (with labels)

● headings

● questions

● bullet points

● short paragraphs

● underlining

● bold text

● capital letters

and anything else which will make your information clear.

But be careful not to confuse your reader with too many styles.

Once you have finished your spread, write a paragraph about how well you think you have achieved your aim. How clear and readable is your page? How might you have made it more informative? What did you find easiest or most difficult as you worked on it?

ASSIGNMENTS

3 Versions of films

Choose a film you really like. Think about your favourite scene and create either:

- a novelisation

or

- a graphic novel.

For the novelisation:

- use plot to say what happens next
- use description to explain what people and places look like
- use speech marks to show the words people say.

For the graphic novel:

- use carefully-chosen images and small amounts of written text – the text should either tell us something about what is happening (for example, 'The next day') or show us the words a character actually says
- use twelve to sixteen image boxes.

Before you start your graphic novel, look back at the example from *The Lost World* – look in particular at the way the image boxes are used. They aren't square boxes side-by-side. Instead the shapes of these boxes add interest and drama to the storyline. If you can, use similar ideas in your sequence.

Finally, whether you chose to create a novelisation or a graphic novel, write a paragraph comparing your version of the film with the original.

1 What problems did you encounter?

2 Which parts of the task were easiest?

3 How have you had to change the story or characters?

4 What differences are there between your version and the original?

Heroines and heroes

Starting points

Most of us admire certain people. They might be people we know –
people in our family or people who have taught us, or people we have
met. Sometimes we know them through the news, or through books –
people in sport, people in history, people who have done things that
have made a difference to the world.

In pairs, or in a small group, think of your own heroines and heroes –
people you admire for their achievements. Try to think of people from
different backgrounds – sports, media, politics and history.

Or you might talk about teachers who have strongly influenced you in
the past – people who you respected and admired and who now, as
you look back, seem like heroines or heroes.

Boy: I saved my pal from canal

The news story on page 37 is from *The Mirror*. It describes a modern-day
hero … and the surprising reaction of his mum. Read the article and then
work through the following activities.

Activities

1 Imagine the scene as Daniel comes
home after saving his friend Luke. He
arrives at the house soaked and dirty,
and his mum immediately thinks he
has been up to mischief.

Either: work in pairs, one of you
playing Daniel and the other his mum.
Make up the conversation that might
have taken place.

Or: write a short script to show what
was said between the two of them.
Use these opening lines as a model:

DANIEL: (shouting) Mum, I'm home.
MUM: About time too. Where've you
been? And what's all this
mess here …?

2 Imagine Luke's reaction to being
saved. In the article he doesn't say
much. Imagine what he would say if
he wrote a letter thanking Daniel for
saving his life. In the letter Luke
might describe what he remembers
about the accident, and then thank
Daniel for being a hero. You could
start like this:

Date here

Dear Daniel
I still can't believe what
happened. One minute we
were just playing, the next…

BOY: I saved my pal from canal
MUM: You're soaked...get to bed

HERO schoolboy Daniel Lilley saved a pal from drowning in a canal – and was sent to bed by his mum for getting wet.

Daniel, 10, came home soaked and dirty after rescuing seven-year-old Luke Jones.

But mum Suzanne thought he had been up to mischief and packed him off to bed early. Yesterday she said: 'It wasn't until the next day when I got calls from the police and his headmaster that I realised he was telling the truth.'

Suzanne, 40, of Wellington Place, Chesterfield, added: 'I've made my apologies now.

'His dad and I are very proud of him.' The boys were playing near Luke's home when the youngster slipped into the murky 6ft deep canal.

Daniel said: 'He was splashing about and calling out for me.

'I could see him going under.

'I can swim, but a policeman who visited our school on Monday told us not to jump after someone who falls in. I couldn't reach Luke at first. He kept slipping away. But he came nearer and I grabbed his hand and was able to pull him out.'

By STEPHEN WHITE

Luke said: 'I can't swim and my face kept going under. Daniel saved me.'

A Derbyshire Police spokesman said: 'Daniel followed our advice, and if it hadn't been for his brave action Luke would have died. He is a hero.'

RESCUED: Luke (left) with hero Daniel

The secret hiding place

The following extract is from a biography. This is a book which tells the story of a person's life. Its subject is Anne Frank, the thirteen-year-old Jewish girl who spent two years hiding from the Nazis in a secret apartment in Amsterdam, Holland. Weeks before the Second World War ended, Anne and her family were discovered and sent to concentration camps. All except her father died there.

The extract describes the Frank family moving to the apartment …

Rain poured down as the Franks, smothered in layers of clothes, hurried through the streets. Jews were forbidden to use the buses; and people in cars, seeing the telltale yellow stars, dared not stop to offer them lifts.

Only now did Anne's parents tell her where they were going. They were
5 to hide inside the old house where Mr Frank had had his office, and where his partners, Mr Kraler and Mr Koophuis, still worked. These two shared the Franks' secret, and so did the secretaries, Miep and Elli.

The tall, thin house, facing the Prinsengracht canal, was a perfect place for hiding. It was like a rabbit warren inside, with its interconnecting rooms,
10 and dark, breakneck staircases. On the ground floor was a warehouse, managed by Elli's father, Mr Vossen. The offices were on the next floor, with storerooms above them; and from the second floor landing a steep staircase led to five tiny back rooms, also on two floors. This was the back wing where the Franks were to live. 'Although it leans to one side and is damp, you'd
15 never find such a comfortable hiding place anywhere in Amsterdam,' Anne wrote in her diary; and she drew a plan so that Kitty could see exactly what it was like. She gave it a name too – the Secret Annexe.

But, coming in out of the rain that first Monday morning, it did not look very comfortable. The little rooms were crammed with
20 boxes, and piles of bedding, stored away over the past few months. Dismayed by the confusion, and wretched at leaving their home, Mrs Frank and Margot gave way. They collapsed onto the unmade beds. But Anne and her father had more courage. Instead of collapsing, they were eager
25 to get things straight.

Curtains were the first essential. If anyone looked out from the houses behind, and saw strange people in the disused wing, they might report them to the Nazis. Quickly Anne and Mr
30 Frank tacked odd strips of material together, and pinned them over the windows. Then, feeling safer, they turned to the boxes. They worked all day, arranging furniture and filling drawers and cupboards. By nightfall the beds were made and the rooms were tidy.

Kitty – the name Anne gave to her diary

35 Anne and Margot shared a tiny bed-room leading off the living-room, where their parents slept. It looked bleak, until Anne brightened it up by sticking post-cards and film star photographs all over
40 the walls. Next door was the bathroom. Upstairs was another small bedroom, and a larger room with a sink and cooker. These were reserved for another family.

45 For, since the Sunday when she had heard they were to hide, Anne had known that some other people were to join them, the Van Daans. Mr Van Daan, who was also a Jew, had been in busi-
50 ness with Mr Frank. He and his wife, with their teenage son, Peter, and their cat, Mouschi, arrived in the Secret Annexe just a week after the Franks, and received a great welcome. At once it
55 was decided that they would all share meals, and live as one large family.

The Van Daans brought interesting news. Early on the morning of the Franks' disappearance, their lodger, Mr
60 Goudsmit, had telephoned Mr Van Daan in alarm. He had found the disordered breakfast table, and the note about the cat, and he could not understand what had happened. He begged Mr Van Daan to come round, which was just what Mr Van Daan was hoping for. He hurried to the house, and,
65 according to a pre-arranged plan, 'discovered' an address jotted down on Mr Frank's writing pad. It was, he told Mr Goudsmit, the address of some friends of the Franks. They lived far away, in a town called Maastricht, and they had once promised to help the Franks. No doubt they had fetched them away in the night.

70 Mr Goudsmit swallowed the story, and so did the neighbours. One lady told Mr Van Daan that she had 'quite definitely' heard a car stop to pick up the Franks in the night. The Frank family sighed with relief. If the Nazis believed they had left Amsterdam, they would not trouble to search for them.

75 But clearly life, even in hiding, would be hazardous. A visitor to the office might find their staircase by chance. So Mr Kraler had a clever idea. He asked Mr Vossen, the warehouseman, to make a bookcase which fitted over the door at the staircase foot. It was hinged, so that it could swing back; but when it was closed, and filled with box files, it looked like part of
80 the office furniture. Nobody could guess what it hid.

The swinging bookcase was only one of the ways in which the hiders were helped by the kind office people. In her diary Anne called them 'the protectors'. Every day they brought food, which was cooked on the stove in the Van Daans' room. Food was rationed, so the protectors had to obtain
85 false ration books, or buy from a few courageous shopkeepers who knew that Jews were hiding in Amsterdam, and who risked their lives to supply them with food.

Without food, of course, the Franks and Van Daans could not have survived, but their protectors brought other things too. They provided clothes,
90 books and newspapers. They lent a radio. Best of all, they simply dropped in to chat. Cooped up in their hiding place, the Franks and Van Daans often felt like prisoners who could not escape. The daily visits of their protectors helped them to feel less forgotten, more in touch with ordinary life as it was going on all the time, outside the walls of the old house by the
95 Amsterdam canal.

Angela Bull, *Anne Frank*

Activities

1 How did the Frank family create the impression that they had left Amsterdam?

2 What picture are we given of Anne Frank's personality? Working in pairs, make a spider diagram to show different sides of her character – like this:

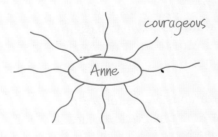

3 Look again at the third paragraph. It shows how cramped the secret annexe is. Yet Anne wrote that 'you'd never find such a comfortable hiding place anywhere in Amsterdam'.

Imagine Anne and her sister first seeing their new bedroom. Anne makes the best of things, but her sister seems less positive. Act or write the conversation that takes place between them. If you write it, set it out as a script. You could start like this:

ANNE: So, here's our new room.
MARGOT: You mean we <u>both</u> have to sleep in here?

The schooldays of Nelson Mandela

Nelson Mandela, President of South Africa, spent twenty-seven years in jail for opposing the racist systems of the country. Released in 1990, he has become probably one of the most respected leaders in the world.

The following extract is from a biography describing his schooldays in one of the separate schools reserved for 'non-white' students.

The white authorities made sure that there were separate schools for whites and blacks, and also separate ones for 'coloureds' and Asians. The government spent at least ten times more on white children than on blacks, and the
5 results were obvious in the schools. Enough money was spent on white schools so that education could be made compulsory. But it wasn't the same for black children, and large numbers never went to school, or dropped out at an early age. Those children, like Nelson Mandela,
10 who actually got as far as high school, belonged to a small élite.

At Healdtown, Nelson was a boarder and was in a dormitory which had little except beds and small lockers for each boy. He was given a mattress cover which
15 he filled with straw to make his bed.

At 6.00 a.m. each morning a wake-up bell rang. After a quick wash in cold water, he had breakfast – a mug of hot water with sugar and a piece of bread. Lunch was the big meal and he ate lots of beans with maize por-
20 ridge, sometimes with a small piece of meat. Supper was the same as breakfast. On Saturdays he could walk the seven miles to the nearest village to buy fish and chips, if he could afford it.

Religion was a strong part of Mandela's life at
25 Healdtown. He had always regularly gone to church and at
Healdtown he took part in the prayers said every evening.
On Sundays, he went to church and to scripture lessons.

In 1938, Nelson Mandela finished his schooling. He had
done so well that Jongintaba decided he should go to uni-
30 versity, to the South African Native College at Fore Hare, not
far from Healdtown. The college was racially segregated.
Most of its three hundred students were blacks, but there
were also 'coloureds' and Asians.

Like any student, Mandela soon discovered that there was
35 much more to being at university than study. He was tall
and good-looking, especially in the three-piece suit tailored
for him. He was popular with women. He took to ballroom
dancing, spending much time learning to waltz and foxtrot.

Benjamin Pogrund, *Nelson Mandela*

Jongintaba – after Nelson Mandela's father
died when Nelson was ten, Chief Jongintaba,
his father's nephew, took responsibility for him

Activities

1 Look again at the paragraphs describing the routine at Healdtown.
Make a list of all the differences from your own school. Are there any
similarities? How would you have coped at a school like Nelson
Mandela's?

2 What impression of the young Nelson Madela's character are we given?

3 If someone was writing a biography about you, what would they say
about your schooldays? How would they describe your:

● school

● daily routine

● attitude to school.

Write two or three paragraphs about yourself, using the third-person
mode (*she* or *he* rather than *I*) to make it sound like an extract from a
biography. Try to show what you are really like at school.

The great magician

The following extract is taken from a reference book and is about a Norse goddess called Freyja. She was famous for her magic, which was designed to create fertility and peace.

Freyja

Norse goddess

The great magician

She was the daughter of Njord and the sister of Freyr. On her chariot drawn by cats 'she is so beautiful that all ornaments are named after her'. She was the wife of Od (holy fury), a god who periodically disappeared for so long that he was believed to be dead, and Freyja shed tears of red gold for him.

Freyja was mistress of *seidr*, a magical science. Its main aims were to know the future and the fates of men, and to cause the seasons and creatures to be fertile. She is linked to the cult of the dead, keepers of wisdom and guardians of the living. 'Wherever she goes in battle she receives half of those who fall, and Odin receives the other half.' She took on the form of a falcon to travel between one world and the other.

Fernande Comte, *Mythologies*

Activities

1 Test your understanding of the text about Freyja.

1 Whose sister was Freyja?

2 What pulled her chariot?

3 Who was her husband?

4 What did he sometimes do?

5 What is the name of the magic science?

6 What was the magic supposed to do?

7 How did she travel between worlds?

2 The extract gives the bare outline of Freyja's life, but little more. Here are two questions you might ask her:

● What does your chariot drawn by cats look like?

● How do you feel each time Od disappears?

Work in pairs to create a two to three minute chat show interview in which we find out more about the character of Freyja.

Start by thinking of the kind of questions the interviewer might ask, and the answers that Freyja might give. One of you be the interviewer and the other Freyja. Rehearse your chat show interview, or script it, if you prefer.

Burn, baby, burn

In 1993, actor Tony Robinson took some of the best-known stories from the Bible and retold them on television. He delivered them to the camera as monologues (a speech given by one person), though he used different voices to play different roles.

Tony Robinson updated the language of the Bible, giving it a very modern, informal feel. But the stories, of heroines and heroes, love and war, bloodshed and peace, remain the same.

The following extract is from the opening of his story about Samuel, the prophet who told people to abandon their old gods and worship the Lord God instead …

"DEATH TO ALL FALSE GODS!" Samuel stood on the mountainside and hurled a statue of the Corn God into the blazing fire.

"Burn, baby, burn," yelled the Israelites.

He wrenched the head off a Thunder God, he broke a statue of the She God across his knee and the pieces went hurtling into the flames. The Israelites were in a frenzy of excitement. "Go! Go! Go!" they yelled.

Meanwhile, deep in the evening shadows, silent figures were creeping towards them. It was a unit of Philistine guerrillas – well armed, well trained and just aching to wipe the smile off the faces of these loud-mouthed, over-bearing Israelites.

"Canaan is our land," roared Samuel. "We were given it by the God of the Israelites."

"Wanna bet?" thought the Philistines and drew their knives.

Kerdoom! A jagged edge of lightning split the sky in two. The whole hillside lit up and suddenly the Philistines were revealed as clear as day.

"Our God has spoken," roared Samuel. "Behold your enemy!"

Boom! A clap of thunder shook the massive mountain. And as the rain began to sheet down, the Israelites yelled their war cry and slithered down the

hillside. The slopes turned to mud, the mud turned to raging streams and soon the Philistines were lost in a torrent of blood and water and charging Israelites.

By the time they got back to Shilo, the Israelites were high as kites. They weren't going to be pushed around any more. "Defend your people! Defend your religion! Defend your territory! Yeahh!!" They wanted their own kingdom – here in Canaan – right now!!

"Hang on," said the milkman. "We'll need a king, won't we?"

"You've already got one," replied Samuel. "The God of the Israelites."

"No," chipped in the fish and chip man, "someone who'll look after us."

"Exactly," answered Samuel.

"Look, stop mucking about" said the vet, and the crossing lady and the man from the garden centre. You know what we mean – a proper king, who'll lead us into battle and stuff."

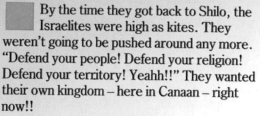

"That'd be great, wouldn't it?" answered Samuel. "Five minutes and you'd be moaning that he was bossing you about."

"No we wouldn't."

"And who'd pay for his palaces, and his wives and all his horrible kids?"

"We would. We wouldn't mind – honest. Come on, Samuel, everyone else's got a king. Come on! Pleeeeeeeease!"

"I'll think about it," said Samuel, and went off to the tent where the Magic Box was kept.

Tony Robinson, *Burn, Baby, Burn: The Story of Samuel*, from 'The Dismembered Camel'

The Real World

Activities

1 The original story of Samuel is thousands of years old. Look closely at the way Tony Robinson updates this text to make it dramatic and attention-grabbing. Look for examples of the way he:

- uses dramatic language
- uses dialogue
- uses references to people who wouldn't really have been around in Biblical times
- uses modern expressions to give it an informal tone.

2 Some readers might say that you shouldn't treat a Bible story in this way. They might argue that Tony Robinson's vesion doesn't treat the story with enough respect or seriousness. What do you think?

3 Tony Robinson's monologue is a really lively, entertaining version of the Bible story. Working in a group of about six, prepare a performance of it, giving out the parts that Tony Robinson originally read himself, to make it into a play. You need the following readers (some people could play more than one part):

- narrator – to read the main storyline (needs to be a confident, dramatic reader)
- Samuel
- milkman
- fish and chip man
- vet/crossing lady/man from the garden centre – all speaking together
- the Philistines – group voices
- the Israelites – group voices.

Spend twenty minutes practising your performance, making sure that:

- the action is fast-moving
- each person reads their part on cue, loudly enough and without long pauses.

ASSIGNMENTS

1 Exceptional people

Anne Frank and Nelson Mandela are two exceptional people who have earned the admiration of millions. Choose someone famous you admire and do some research about:

- their background and early years
- schooldays
- early adult life
- achievements.

You could use encyclopaedias, biographies, CD-ROMs, the Internet and newspapers to help you research.

Then write an interview between yourself and your chosen person, asking questions and giving answers which tell everyone about their life.

2 Personal heroes

Think of someone in your own life who has had a powerful influence upon you and whom you admire – a friend, relative, teacher or other adult you have known.

Write a mini-biography of them, showing what they are like:

- their appearance
- their way of talking
- their background
- their personal qualities for example, whether they are brave, thoughtful ...
- some specific memories of things they have done.

Add a final paragraph describing why they have had such an influence upon you.

3 Old tales

Choose a traditional tale that you know well, such as a Greek myth, local legend, or story from the Bible. Retell it in a lively, modern and dramatic way, just as Tony Robinson does with the story of Samuel. Aim to:

- use dramatic words and phrases
- use dialogue for different characters. You can use characters you have made up (as Tony Robinson does with the vet, lollipop lady, and so on)
- use informal language, so that it feels like a story to be spoken aloud rather than read silently.

Stories you could use include:

- Freyja, the great magician
- Jonah and the whale
- David and Goliath
- Hercules.

Food, glorious food

Starting points

This unit contains a variety of different texts on the theme of food, and looks at different attitudes to what we eat.

Look at the comments below and, for each one, decide whether you agree or disagree:

Comment	Agree	Disagree	Not sure
1 We cannot live without food.			
2 Most people in our society eat too much.			
3 School canteens should only serve food which is healthy.			
4 We should not eat food which involves harming living organisms (animals and plants).			
5 People should be allowed to eat whatever food they want.			

Now, working in pairs or in a small group, spend three minutes comparing your responses. Find out:

● which comment(s) you all agree with

● which comment is the most controversial (difficult to agree upon).

Healthy eating for the elderly

The leaflet on pages 49–52, was created for Tesco supermarkets. It aims to give advice to the elderly about eating a healthy diet.

As you read, think about what is being said, and decide how successful you think it is. If you were an elderly person, would you find the information helpful?

EAT TO BE FIT

No matter what your age, eating a healthy, balanced diet is important. More people are living longer and many elderly people enjoy a healthy, active life. In later years though, your dietary requirements change and this leaflet looks at the main issues involved in keeping fit and well in retirement.

When you get to retirement age, eating a diet that is aimed at preventing diseases may seem irrelevant. But there are many reasons for eating a healthy, balanced diet: - maintaining the right weight for your height; - for a healthy blood and nervous system; - for a healthy digestive system.
"A little of what you fancy does you good."
Ageing can lead to all sorts of problems - physical as well as economic. Problems with dentures or getting out to do the shopping can lead to a disinterest in food. And if you are worried about what the right thing is to eat you could be restricting your diet.
The main message is to keep an interest in food and enjoy cooking and eating. There is no such thing as unhealthy food, just an unhealthy diet.

WHAT'S IMPORTANT IN YOUR DIET?

Eating a wide variety of foods is still important. Meals should be based on starchy carbohydrates such as bread, potatoes, pasta and rice, with at least 5 portions of fruit and vegetables a day. Add to that lean meats, skinless poultry, fish or pulses and some milk and dairy products. This is the basis of a healthy balanced diet for anyone, but the elderly need to keep an eye on a few other areas:

ENERGY

Eating enough to maintain a steady body weight is important. Being underweight can increase your risk of disease and being overweight affects your mobility and general well-being. A diet low in calories may be low in other nutrients too.

FATS

It is still important to keep an eye on your total fat and saturated fat intake, to reduce your risk of heart disease. Certain fats such as Omega-3 polyunsaturates, which may have a beneficial effect on blood clotting, should be increased. These are found in oily fish. Cutting down on fat is a good way to cut out calories, which is important if you are overweight. But you still need some fat to provide fat-soluble vitamins and essential fatty acids.

tips

1. Always grill meats and sausages rather than frying them. Trim off any excess fat before cooking.

2. If you do fry, use a little sunflower oil. With many meats there is no need to add any extra fat. Cook over a low heat to start with to release the natural fat to fry in. Drain foods well before serving.

3. Keep a supply of canned fish such as tuna or sardines. Sardines make a very good lunch dish on wholemeal toast or used as a jacket potato filling.

4. Poached fruit such as apples, pears, plums and peaches makes an ideal dessert. Peel, core and slice. Poach in a little fruit juice such as apple or orange. Freeze any left over for another day.

5. Add extra chopped vegetables such as celery, carrots, mushrooms or garden peas to stews and casseroles. Or add mashed swede or carrot to mashed potatoes.

6. Unsalted nuts make a very good snack or add them chopped to homemade stuffings, toppings on cottage pies and desserts.

7. Stir-fry dishes are quick to make and save on washing up. Stir-fry thin strips of beef or chicken with lots of colourful vegetables such as carrots, leeks, broccoli, courgettes and french beans in a large frying pan.

For any advice on food and health write to:
Food Advice Service, Tesco Stores Ltd,
P.O. Box 18, Cheshunt, Herts EN8 9SL.

Activities

1 What picture of elderly people does the leaflet give – fit, enthusiastic, lively, slowing down, worried? Think of one word which you think best describes them, and find a sentence from the leaflet which supports your opinion.

2 Look at the way the leaflet is presented. Consider the use of:

- images (what kinds of pictures are included?)
- headings (is the style chatty, serious, joky, factual …?)
- typefaces (large, small, modern, plain, fancy? Why?).

Do you think these design features work well in making it easy to read and attractive to look at? What changes would you make to improve it?

3 How would you present the information differently for a younger audience – say aged eleven to sixteen? Use a sheet of A4 paper to design your leaflet. Remember to:

- make a rough version first, to get the layout right
- use different visual features to add interest – short paragraphs, bullet points, questions, headings, different typefaces
- choose images that will appeal to your younger audience. Don't worry if you think you can't draw well: just sketch an outline and then label the picture to say what you are trying to show.

4 How would an elderly person feel about the Tesco leaflet? Would s/he find it helpful, interesting, insulting, irrelevant? Imagine you are over sixty and have recently picked up the leaflet. Write a letter to the manager of your local store giving your opinions about the leaflet. You might start like this:

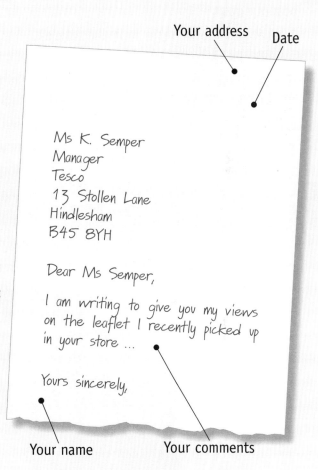

Your address   Date

Ms K. Semper
Manager
Tesco
13 Stollen Lane
Hindlesham
B45 8YH

Dear Ms Semper,

I am writing to give you my views on the leaflet I recently picked up in your store …

Yours sincerely,

Your name   Your comments

Tried and tasted

The article on page 55 is taken from a Sunday newspaper. It gives the results of a taste test on different brands of peanut butter. Its aim is to help readers decide which brands have the best taste and offer the best value.

Read the article and then work through the following activities.

Activities

1 Check your understanding of the text on peanut butter.

1 What *facts* do we learn from the article about peanuts and peanut butter? Make a list.

2 Which brands do best in the taste test and which do worst? Compare the descriptions.

3 What other tests would have been useful?

2 Look again at the introduction to the taste test. It gives a quick history of peanut butter. Do you think this is a good way to lead into the survey, or is it too factual? How would you have introduced the test?

3 Working in a group of three or four, carry out your own taste test on different brands of these products:

• baked beans

• low-fat crisps

• sugar-free orange squash

• yoghurt.

1 Decide what features you will examine in your test.

2 Decide how you will rate each feature (star system? marks out of five?).

3 Organise the test, either to complete in a lesson, or at home.

4 Write up your results, perhaps using graphs or charts to make them clearer to your readers. You could then present the results to the rest of the class.

TRIED & TASTED
CRUNCHY PEANUT BUTTER

The invention of peanut butter is credited to Dr John Kellogg (brother of the founder of the Kellogg's cereal company) in the late 1890s, who is said to have been looking for a concentrated high protein and energy food for elderly patients at his Michigan sanatorium.

Peanuts are high in oil, so peanut butter is high in calories – there are about 120 in a heaped 20-gramme teaspoonful.

Peanut butter must contain at least 90% peanuts, which are roasted and skinned, then ground to a paste with additional oil. The mixture may have emulsifiers,

and oils, salt and sugar (or apple juice) may be added.

More than half of the £24m worth of peanut butter consumed last year in Britain was crunchy, with smooth making up just under 40% and the relatively new wholenut varieties about 7%.

The Sunday Times panel tasted the most widely available brands of crunchy peanut butter and awarded each product a star rating to a maximum of five. The panel were looking for a predominantly savoury, lightly salted taste, but with a hint of sweetness.

Janette Marshall

★★★★★ **Sun-Pat Crunchy Peanut Butter** (59p/227g, 84p/340g from supermarkets and independent grocers). 'Strong freshly roasted peanut flavour', 'appetising mixture of sweet and savoury tastes', 'lots of crunch in a smooth but not cloying butter – very pleasant'.

★★★★★ **Asda Crunchy Peanut Butter** (57p/227g). 'Delicious dark-roasted peanut flavour and colour', 'rich and warm, not too sticky', 'plenty of crunch'.

★★★★★ **Safeway Crunchy Peanut Butter** (57p/227g, 79p/340g). 'Good rich colour and strong nutty flavour', 'fairly thick with good crunch', 'not too clinging'.

★★★★★ **Golden Country Natural Crunchy Peanut Butter** (57p/227g from Gateway). 'Appealing golden-roasted colour and glossy sheen', 'good balance of salty, savoury taste and sweetness', 'fresh tasting with lots of crunch'.

The Sunday Times Choice
Sun-Pat Crunchy

★★★★★ **Tesco Crunchy Peanut Butter** (57p/227g). 'Rich, glossy colour', 'fresh savoury aroma', 'hint of sweetness, good peanut flavour but maybe a bit too dry and sticky'.

★★★★ **Sainsbury's Crunchy Peanut Butter** (57p/227g, 79p/340g). 'Good, pleasant flavour but too sticky and coats the roof of the mouth', 'not quite crunchy enough'.

★★ **Waitrose Crunchy Peanut Butter** (79p/340g). 'Very pale, thick and dry looking, but lots of crunchy chopped peanuts', 'more sweet than salty with odd pasty texture', 'poor peanut flavour'.

★★ **Whole Earth Original Crunchy Peanut Butter** (85p/312g from health food shops and some supermarkets). 'Pale and flecked with bits of red peanut skin', 'strong nutty smell, but peanuts taste a bit raw'.

★ **KP Crunchy Peanut Butter** (about 52p/227g, 76p/340g from supermarkets and independent grocers). 'Extremely smooth, glossy paste with chopped nuts', 'very odd whipped, mousse-like texture', 'peanut flavour good, but too sweet and bland'.

★ **Whole Earth American Style Crunchy Peanut Butter**, (89p/302g from health food shops and some supermarkets). 'Pale and thick, and dry rather than glossy', 'strong oily smell', 'too sweet, more like a paste than a butter', 'not crunchy enough, and raw tasting'.

Tasting held at Leith's School of Food & Wine.

sanatorium – place for the care of long-term patients

Eating out

The following article is a review of a restaurant from a local newspaper. Reviews are intended to entertain and inform the reader. Read what the reviewer thinks of the food and service at this restaurant.

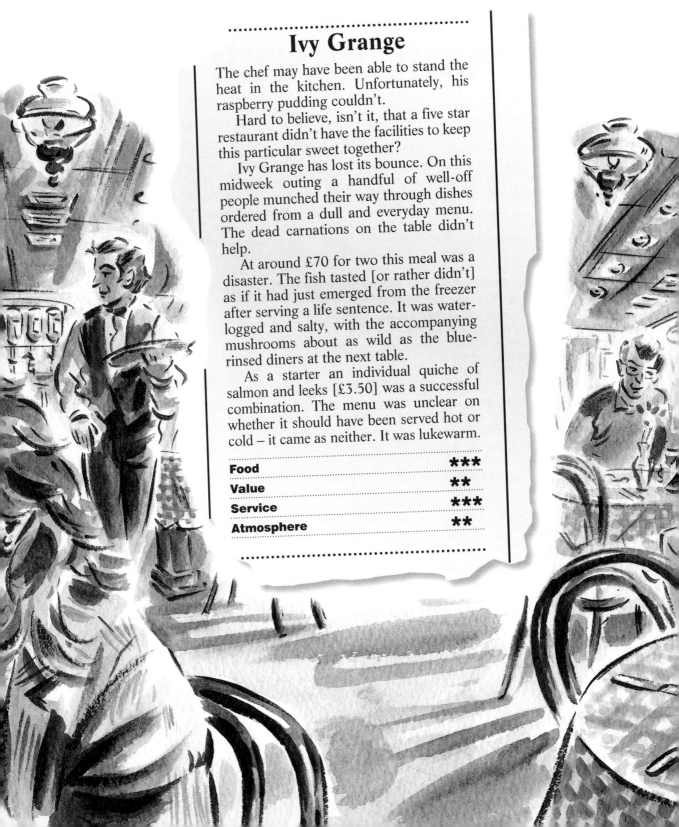

Ivy Grange

The chef may have been able to stand the heat in the kitchen. Unfortunately, his raspberry pudding couldn't.

Hard to believe, isn't it, that a five star restaurant didn't have the facilities to keep this particular sweet together?

Ivy Grange has lost its bounce. On this midweek outing a handful of well-off people munched their way through dishes ordered from a dull and everyday menu. The dead carnations on the table didn't help.

At around £70 for two this meal was a disaster. The fish tasted [or rather didn't] as if it had just emerged from the freezer after serving a life sentence. It was water-logged and salty, with the accompanying mushrooms about as wild as the blue-rinsed diners at the next table.

As a starter an individual quiche of salmon and leeks [£3.50] was a successful combination. The menu was unclear on whether it should have been served hot or cold – it came as neither. It was lukewarm.

Food	***
Value	**
Service	***
Atmosphere	**

Activities

1 Find a sentence which you think is intended to entertain the reader. Find a sentence which you think is intended to inform.

2 Which parts of the text do you find funny? Do any parts seem cruel? How does the writer try to make us laugh?

3 Write a humorous review of a meal you have eaten in your school canteen. Aim to entertain your readers by writing it as if you were at an expensive restaurant. You might begin:

> My partner and I had heard great things about this place. There was a long queue — usually a sign that the place is popular and the food is good ...

4 Imagine you are the chef at Ivy Grange. You think the review is unfair. Write a letter to the reviewer saying why you don't like the style of the review. You might begin:

> Name
>
> Dear
>
> I have just finished reading your review of my restaurant, Ivy Grange. I have to say I am furious at the way you have described us. Allow me to explain ...

Milked for all she's worth

The following leaflet aims to persuade the reader that the treatment of dairy cattle is cruel. Look at the way the writer uses facts and opinions to persuade the reader.

MILKED FOR ALL SHE'S WORTH

The dairy cow grazing peacefully in the fields masks a tale of gross exploitation:

- Pregnant for 9 months of every year, milked for 10 months of every year.
- Her calf is taken from her at 1–3 days old.
- She is milked to capacity, producing 10 times as much milk as her calf would have drunk – had it been left to suckle.
- To increase her milk yield she is fed high protein concentrates – too many concentrates can lead to acidosis and lameness – 25% of dairy cows suffer from lameness every year.
- Machine milking and indoor cubicle housing predispose the cow to mastitis – inflammation of the udder. Every year mastitis hits one-third of our dairy cows.
- Research is now being done to enable the dairy farmer to inject his cows daily with bovine growth hormone, to make them produce more milk.
- By the time they are $7\frac{1}{2}$ years old three-quarters of our dairy cows will be slaughtered, worn out with the strains of production.

WHAT YOU CAN DO:

- Ask your MP to object to the licensing of bovine growth hormone.
- Send for our Fact Sheet on Cattle (50p).
- Send for our Cruelty-free Diet Sheet (50p).
- Try some alternatives to dairy products: soya milk, vegetable margarine, tofu (soya curd cheese).

Send coupon below to:
Tel: (01730) 264208
COMPASSION IN WORLD FARMING, 5a Charles Street, Petersfield, Hants GU32 3EH

I enclose 50p for a cattle fact sheet/cruelty-free diet sheet ❏
I enclose .... as a donation to CIWF ❏
I enclose £7 for annual membership of CIWF ❏
Name:..
Address:..
....
....

Activities

1 Which of the facts in the leaflet did you already know? Which do you find most surprising, disturbing or shocking?

2 How well do you think the picture works? Can you think of a better image?

3 Look more closely at the language of the leaflet. Do you agree with this response from Kelly in Year 8? Support your ideas with examples.

'I found the words difficult to follow. They're quite technical. I think the writer could have written in a more straightforward style'.

4 If you were trying to give the same message through a 30-second radio commercial, what would you say? What words would you use and what sound effects? Remember: you want to persuade your listeners that over-milking of cows is cruel.

You could:

- use a direct style
('Listen to some facts about ...')

- use a sketch style
(VOICE 1: Morning Bill. Time to check on the herd again is it?
VOICE 2: That's right Pete ...)

- use a hard-hitting reporting style
(sounds of countryside; confused noises; reporter: 'I'm about to join milking time down on the farm and I can tell you, it's not going to be pleasant'; quietly, as if in distance: 'Get off my land ...').

5 Imagine how a dairy farmer might feel about the message of the leaflet. S/he might feel angry at the idea that everyone should switch to something like soya milk. Write a letter or leaflet to persuade readers to keep using dairy products (you could mention the natural ingredients and their freshness).

If you design a leaflet, produce a draft first, then look at some of the leaflets presented in other units of this book (pages 49–52, 90–91). Notice the design and the kind of language they use.

ASSIGNMENTS

1 Food for thought

Organise a debate on the way humans use animals for food. You could discuss dairy farming, fishing, other forms of factory farming or hunting. Begin with a statement such as: 'We believe that modern farming methods are cruel'. Some people should speak agreeing with the statement, others disagreeing. Start like this:

- Decide what you believe and which side you are on.

- Gather the facts and information to support your view.

- Write a one to two minute speech explaining your case – but remember that this will need to do more than just contain a list of the facts you have gathered. You will need to *persuade* your audience to agree with you. Use emotional words, repeat key ideas, ask questions to make people think ('Is this really a fair way to treat animals ...?').

Now write up the debate in a report.

Continued on page 60

ASSIGNMENTS

2 Fact file

Continued from page 59

On one side of A4 paper, produce your own fact sheet for healthy living. Decide precisely what group of people it is aimed at. Use language which will make your information clear. You could:

- use short paragraphs
- use questions
- use headings and subheadings to add clarity
- use the style sheets below for hints on how to design it
- put some text in panels or boxes to highlight key points.

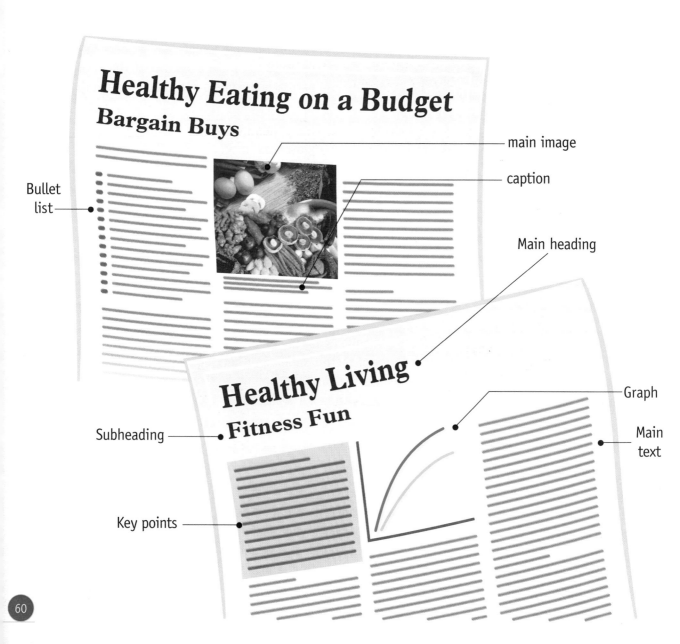

Mysteries of the unexplained

We like to think we can explain most of what happens in the world. Science, technology and communications have helped us to understand how things work. But some parts of life continue to baffle us, and some people still turn to horoscopes or fortune-telling in search of answers. Then there are the sightings of UFOs, of strange, unknown creatures, of prehistoric monsters in Scottish lochs … These are just a few mysteries of the unexplained!

On the trail of the Fen Tiger

In the city of Cambridge there are reports of a creature on the loose. People call it the Fen Tiger because it seems to live on the fens – the marshy flatlands outside the city. Is it a tiger or wolf, or some strange throwback to a creature that stalked the land long ago?

Read the report on page 62 from the local newspaper, *The Cambridge Evening News*, then work through the following activities.

Activities

1 What do you think of the headline of this article? Do you think it is too joky for a serious story? If so, what headline would you have given the article?

2 Imagine a programme like *Crimewatch* which aims to warn viewers about the mystery animal. It might create a reconstruction of when the beast was last spotted. It might then talk to different eye-witnesses about what they thought they saw.

In groups of four, put together a four- to five-minute programme. You could call it *Fenwatch*. Try to keep the tone serious so that it seems real. Amongst the characters you might include are: the presenter, one or two eye-witnesses, an expert (for example, a professor of zoology – the study of animals) to help explain what the creature might be.

You could include artists' impressions of what the eyewitnesses thought they saw.

Improvise or script the programme and then present it to the rest of the class.

Fen Tiger is secret pigeon fancier

■ **CAMBRIDGE:** The Fen Tiger is on the prowl again, says a university night porter who claims he saw the big cat munching pigeons in college grounds.

Shaun Pleasants, who works at St John's College, saw a large animal 'like a lynx' when he went to unlock a bridge over the river at 6am on Sunday.

And the 30-year-old, of Maitland Avenue, Cambridge, said it was the second time in less than a month the animal had been seen in college grounds.

He said: 'It was black and looked like a lynx. it was smaller than a big dog and had a black long tail.

'It definitely wasn't a fox – it was light and I could see it quite clearly. It was crouching down eating something.

'When it saw me it turned and ran off and jumped across the stream. There was part of a pigeon and another headless one lying on the ground.

'I was a bit scared … but when it saw me it looked more scared of me than anything.'

He said another porter claimed to have seen the beast in the bushes at Fellows Garden last month.

Again, there were remains of pigeons on the grass.

Now Mr Pleasants believes the cat regularly comes to feed on the birds at dawn when they fly on to the grass to look for worms.

'We are thinking of getting a cheap camera and seeing if we can catch it on film,' he added.

'We are always finding dead pigeons.'

Sightings of sea monsters

The Loch Ness monster isn't the only creature to have been 'seen' by humans. The following extracts contain accounts of various strange sightings in the lakes and seas of the world.

MONSTERS OF LAKES AND SEAS

BEFORE 1900

'Incontestibly the largest Sea-monster in the world' was described by Erik L. Pontoppidan, Bishop of Bergen, in *The Natural History of Norway* (1752-53). The kraken, as fishermen and the bishop called it, was so enormous that even when it surfaced its whole body did not appear. Wrote Pontoppidan:

'... its back or upper part, which seems to be in appearance about an English mile and a half in circumference, (some say more, but I choose the least for greater certainty) looks at first like a number of small islands, surrounded with something that floats and fluctuates like sea weeds ... at last several bright points or horns appear, which grow thicker and thicker the higher they rise above the surface of the water, and sometimes they stand up as high and large as the masts of middle-siz'd vessels.

It seems these are the creature's arms, and, it is said, if they were to lay hold of the largest man-of-war, they would pull it down to the bottom.'

Bernard Heuvelmans, *In the Wake of the Sea-Serpents*

In July 1734 a Norwegian missionary named Hans Egede, voyaging to Greenland, spotted something incredible as his vessel neared the Danish colony of Good Hope on the Davis Strait. 'On the 6th,' as he subsequently reported in straightforward terms,

'appeared a very terrible sea-animal, which raised itself so high above the water, that its head reached above our maintop. It had a long, sharp snout, and blew like a whale, had broad, large flappers, and the body was, as it were, covered with a hard skin, and it was very wrinkled and uneven on its skin; moreover on the lower part it was formed like a snake, and when it went under water again, it cast itself backwards, and in doing so it raised its tail above the water, a whole ship-length from its body. That evening we had very bad weather.'

Richard Carrington, *Mermaids and Mastodons*

A sea serpent of impressive size was reportedly seen in and around Gloucester Harbour, Massachusetts, by many persons during the month of August 1817. Prompted by heated debate between believers and skeptics, a special committee of the Linnaean Society of New England collected a sheaf of sworn statements from purported eyewitnesses. The affidavit of Matthew Gaffney, ship's carpenter, typically deposed:

'That on the 14th day of August, AD 1817, between the hours of four and five o'clock in the afternoon, I saw a strange marine animal, resembling a serpent in the harbour in said Gloucester. I was in a boat, and was within 30 feet of him. His head appeared full as large as a four-gallon keg, his body as large as a barrel, and his length that I saw I should judge 40 feet at least. The top of his head was of a dark color, and the underpart of his head appeared nearly white, as did also several feet of his belly that I saw ... I fired at him when he was the nearest to me.'

The creature, Gaffney went on, turned as if to charge the boat, then sank like a stone and re-appeared some 100 yards away. It moved at a rate of about one mile per two or three minutes.

Reader's Digest, eds., *American Folklore and Legend*

incontestibly – without question
fluctuates – rises and falls like waves
skeptics – those who are doubtful, questioning
purported – apparent
affidavit – a statement written down and sworn to be true
deposed – testified

Capt. Peter M'Quhae and most of the officers and crew of H.M.S. *Daedalus* were treated to the sight of 'a sea-serpent of extraordinary dimensions' while on passage from the East Indies to Plymouth, England, in 1848. In a detailed, matter-of-fact statement dated October 11, Captain M'Quhae advised the lords of the admiralty that at 5 p.m. on August 6 – the *Daedalus* then being in the South Atlantic 300 miles off the western coast of Africa – 'something very unusual was seen by Mr. Sartoris, midshipman, rapidly approaching the ship from behind the beam.'

Mr. Sartoris immediately reported the circumstance to Captain M'Quhae and two officers walking the quarterdeck. What they and several other incredulous viewers saw was an enormous, undulating, snakelike thing 'with head and shoulders kept about four feet constantly above the surface of the sea.' As nearly as the men could judge by making a comparison with the length of their main topsail yard, the serpent's visible length was a good 60 feet, its diameter behind the head was 15 or 16 inches, and there seemed to be some kind of mane down the creature's back.

incredulous – unbelieving
appendage – something added or attached

It must have been a vastly surprised Mr. Hoad of Adelaide, Australia, who, while walking along Brungle Creek one day in the early fall of 1883, came upon the remains of an unworldly creature. The thing was piglike in form, with a headless trunk and an appendage that curved inward like the tail of a lobster. Needless to say, it has never been identified.

Charles Fort, *The Complete Books of Charles Fort*

FROM 1900 TO 1970

Surveying the Amazon basin for the Royal Geographical Society of London in 1907, Maj. Percy Fawcett could not at first credit local tales of out-size snakes inhabiting the swamps and rivers. But, as he was to write in his memoirs, personal experience convinced him they were true. Fawcett and his Indian crew were slowly drifting down the sluggish Rio Abuná when, almost under the bow of their flimsy boat,

(… there appeared a triangular head and several feet of undulating body. It was a giant anaconda. I sprang for my rifle as the creature began to make its way up the bank, and hardly waiting to aim, smashed a .44 soft-nosed bullet into its spine, ten feet below the wicked head. At once there was a flurry of foam, and several heavy thumps against the boat's keel, shaking us as though we had run on a snag … We stepped ashore and approached the reptile with caution. It was out of action, but shivers ran up and down my body like puffs of wind on a mountain tarn. As far as it was possible to measure, a length of forty-five feet lay out of the water, and seventeen feet in it, making a total length of sixty-two feet.)

On a return trip to London, Fawcett was branded a liar for his claim that he had bagged a 62-foot anaconda. That animal, scientists declared, could not possibly measure more than about 45 feet; therefore the observer's story was fantastic.

Bernard Heuvelmans, *On the Track of Unknown Animals*

anaconda – large snake which kills its prey by constriction

Activities

1 In pairs, discuss:

- which of these sightings of sea monsters seem most similar
- which you find most believable and why
- which you find most unbelievable and why.

2 Choose one of the monster sightings and use the description to draw a picture of what the creature might have looked like. Label your illustration to show the different details.

3 Imagine you are a news reporter interviewing one or two of the eyewitnesses about what they saw. Think of the questions you will ask them.

Either: work in pairs to improvise an interview.

Or: write it out as a script.

You might start like this:

INTERVIEWER: I am joined here today by (name of eyewitness). Describe to us what you were doing just before the sighting.

EYEWITNESS: We were just sailing along. It was just like any other normal day …

The night flyer of Talyllyn

Everyone has a favourite story of a place or building that's haunted.

Why do you think people love to hear, read, or watch ghost stories? What kinds of buildings are usually thought of as haunted? Are there some places that you could never imagine as the settings for ghost stories, such as supermarkets or swimming pools?

A popular short story by the nineteenth century novelist, Charles Dickens, is *The Signalman*. It is a spine-chilling tale about a ghostly railway line. Railways have often attracted mysterious rumours and legends. Look at the following account – said to be true – about a mysterious locomotive in South Wales.

The Night Flyer of Talyllyn

The Welsh town of Tywyn, facing out across the beautiful sweep of Cardigan Bay, is one of those lovely spots that, once visited, are never forgotten. Beyond the town, running to the north-east, is the famous old Talyllyn Railway.

This whole area of Wales is replete with legends and stories of strange nocturnal happenings, so it is hardly surprising to learn that the Talyllyn Railway is haunted, too. Weird lights have been reported on the line long after the last train has run, and the harsh whistle of an engine has been heard on certain stretches, especially near the viaduct at Dolgoch.

Seen by day from the B4405 which runs beside the railway for half its length, the Dolgoch Viaduct is an impressive-looking construction. By night, however, it has a strangely eerie quality, and to walk over it is to sense the great antiquity of the Welsh fastness all around. Indeed, locals say it takes stout-hearted men and women to be about in Dolgoch after night falls.

But such bravery is precisely what a group of climbers from an outdoor pursuits centre showed when they asked for permission to abseil down Dolgoch Viaduct at midnight one autumn evening in 1982. According to one report, as they were tying their ropes to the rails on the viaduct in preparation for their descent, a dark, mysterious shape hurtled at them out of the darkness.

No one among the group was quite sure what they saw, for it all happened so quickly. Whether it was something real or intangible was impossible to say; but the shape of the 'thing', and the fact they were on the railway, made them think it must be a locomotive of some kind. Although the group were somewhat shaken by their experience, they nonetheless abseiled down the viaduct and later reported their strange experience in Tywyn.

To the local people, the story merely added weight to the long-held belief that the line was haunted, and a newspaper later carried an account which began, 'Strange nocturnal happenings have confirmed the existence of a ghost train on the Talyllyn Railway.'

There was, though, another suggestion: that the 'ghost train' might actually have been a runaway trolley hi-jacked by pranksters to frighten the abseilers – but this did not explain the dramatic disappearance of the 'thing' over the edge of the viaduct, nor the fact that nothing whatsoever was found anywhere on the line between the viaduct and Tywyn.

Richard Peyton, *The Book of Great Mysteries*

replete – full
antiquity – age
fastness – vast, empty, dark and quiet space
abseiling – descending a steep or verticle surface using ropes
confirmed – supported or agreed with

Activities

1 The account of the 'ghost train' is presented as true. What makes it seem as if it might be true? Is there anything which makes you think that it is made up? Look for:

- names of places
- amount of detail
- descriptions from eyewitnesses
- the writer's style.

Then list your points in two columns, like this:

Could be true	Probably made up

2 The extract doesn't really tell us much about what the abseilers saw on the viaduct that midnight in 1982. Imagine you were one of the group who took part. You saw something. You couldn't believe your eyes. You hurried nervously home. What did you write as a diary entry for that evening?

Think yourself into the role and write about what happened. Start with your arrival for the abseiling. Describe what you and the other abseilers were doing. Then show how this unexplained event occurred and what finally happened.

The walking dead

Corpses which get up and walk around are known as zombies.
The extract which follows is taken from a reference book which
gives information about another strange mystery of the unexplained …

The walking dead

'The eyes were the worst. It was not my imagination. They
were in truth like the eyes of a dead man, not blind, but
staring, unfocused, unseeing. The whole face, for that
matter, was bad enough. It was vacant, as if there was
5 nothing behind it. It seemed not only expressionless, but
incapable of expression. I had seen so much previously in
Haiti that was outside ordinary normal experience that for
the flash of a second I had a sickening, almost panicky
lapse in which I thought, or rather felt, 'Great God, maybe
10 this stuff is really true …'

This was how William Seabrook described his
encounter with one of the most horrifying creatures ever
to step from the realms of the supernatural. For Seabrook
was face-to-face with a zombie – a walking corpse. And in
15 that moment he was prepared to believe all he had heard
about zombies since he first arrived on the island of Haiti.

The zombie's fate is even worse than that of the vampire or the werewolf. The vampire returns to his loved ones. He may be recognized and lain to rest. The werewolf
20 may be wounded and regain human form. But the zombie is a mindless automaton, doomed to live out a twilight existence of brutish toil. A zombie can move, eat, hear, even speak, but he has no memory of his past or knowledge of his present condition. He may pass by his
25 own home or gaze into the eyes of his loved ones without a glimmer of recognition.

Neither ghost nor person, the zombie is said to be trapped, possibly forever, in that 'misty zone that divides life from death'. For while the vampire is the living dead,
30 the zombie is merely the walking dead – a body without soul or mind raised from the grave and given a semblance of life through sorcery. He is the creature of the sorcerer, who uses him as a slave or hires him out – usually to work on the land.

Ed. Colin Wilson and Christopher Evans, *The Book of Great Mysteries*

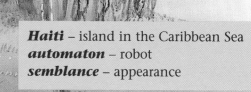

Haiti – island in the Caribbean Sea
automaton – robot
semblance – appearance

Activities

1 The extract gives a definition of a zombie. Design a spider diagram around the word *zombie* to show the key features of these creatures.

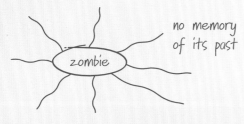

no memory of its past

zombie

2 William Seabrook was clearly disturbed by what he saw. He describes his encounter with the zombie, but gives little information about where it took place or what happened next.

Work in pairs. One of you imagine yourself into the role of William Seabrook. The other is an interviewer. Find out more about William Seabrook's strange sighting, either by improvising or scripting a drama.

What are vampires?

The following extract is from a textbook about unexplained mysteries. It attempts to explain how the legend of vampires began. According to the extract there are several explanations as to why people think they have encountered vampires ...

VAMPIRES

Without wishing to pour cold water (or garlic juice!) on the idea of the vampire, there are a number of simple reasons which explain the legend. Dennis Wheatley, author of such thrillers as *The Devil Rides Out*, has a convincing theory that in
5 times of extreme poverty beggars would make their homes in graveyards, emerging from tombs in the cover of darkness to scavenge for food. If they were seen in the moonlight, stealing out of coffins, it is not very surprising that rumours would be spread quickly by word of mouth from person to person, then
10 from village to village, until the seeds of the legend would be sown over an entire district.

There is another obvious theory which explains a great deal – that vampires were really unfortunate people who had been buried alive. Premature, burial has taken place on occasions
15 right up to the present day, for the simple reason that a state of death is extremely difficult to certify. In 1885, the *British Medical Journal* stated, 'It is true that hardly any one sign of death, short of putrefaction, can be relied on as infallible.' This is just as true today – for without sophisticated clinical tests,
20 you can only really be certain that death has occurred when the body begins to decay. In fact, you can still occasionally read of the terrible shock that befalls an unlucky mortuary attendant when he finds that one of his corpses is still alive.

32

premature – too early
putrefaction – rotting away
infallible – always right

A number of Victorians were terrified of being buried alive.
25 Wilkie Collins, who wrote two of the first and most famous thrillers – *The Moonstone* and *The Woman in White* – left instructions for various tests to be made before he was buried, so that there should be no doubt that he was dead. A Russian, Count Karnicki, invented a coffin with a glass ball resting on
30 top of the body. If the corpse moved, the ball released a spring and the lid would fly open while a flag waved above and a bell rang for assistance. This contraption sounds pretty silly, but Collins and Karnicki had a point when you consider that at least one person was buried alive every week in America at the
35 beginning of this century!

One such victim was a young woman who lived near Indianapolis. When she collapsed, six doctors signed the death certificate after making the usual tests, but her young brother refused to believe them. He tried to prevent her body being
40 removed for the funeral several days later, and in the struggle a bandage came loose around her jaw and it could be seen that her lips were moving.

'What do you want, what do you want?' cried the boy.

'Water,' she whispered faintly. She revived and lived to an
45 old age.

Another American woman, the respected matron of a large orphanage, was declared dead and her body placed in a shroud before she was rescued and revived by friends. Needless to say, extra precautions were taken the next time she was presumed
50 to be dead, but again her body was shrouded. Luckily, the undertaker happened to pierce her body with a pin, and noticed that a small drop of blood oozed from the puncture, to the joy of her friends who helped her recover. These women were fortunate – just imagine the numbers of people who were
55 not rescued in time. It is a grisly thought.

33

Daniel Farson, *The Beaver Book of Horror*

Activities

1 The article contains two main theories about the legend of vampires. Skim the text and summarize these theories, using a table like the one below:

Theory	Summary of theory

2 Look again at the description of Count Karnicki's invention. Using the details in the text, sketch what you think his invention would have looked like.

3 Based on the vampire text:

Either: write an interview with the woman from near Indianapolis who escaped just before being buried alive. Look at the details:

- Six doctors pronounced her dead. Could she hear what they were saying?

- A bandage was tied round her jaw. What was she feeling?

- Her brother refused to accept the tests. Could she hear the argument?

- The bandage around her jaw loosened and she spoke. How did she feel?

Or: interview the woman mentioned in the next paragraph, who was revived just before burial.

In your interview questions, focus on what the women remember and what their feelings were. You could start like this:

INTERVIEWER: You have been through an extraordinary experience. What is the first thing you remember?

WOMAN: I can't remember much, but I do remember hearing voices. People were talking about me, saying I was dead, and there was nothing I could do ...

ASSIGNMENTS

1 Beastly sighting

Imagine there has been a sighting of an unexplained beast in an area you know well. Think what the creature might look like, what it might do and where it might be seen. How would your local newspaper report the news? Write the first two hundred words of the article.

Remember to:

- use the first sentence to give a summary of the whole story
- give details about the creature and where it was seen
- use eyewitness reports (short quotations) in your article
- write in a serious tone – don't turn the event into a joke.

2 Ghost train

Take the account of the abseilers of Talyllyn and make it into a spine-chilling story.

1 First think of your main characters – their names, backgrounds, and where they live.

2 Describe the beginning of their trip as they start abseiling.

3 Describe the first signs that everything is not normal – sounds or sights of a train.

4 Describe your characters' reactions.

5 What happens next ...?

3 Horror stories

Imagine you are working on a magazine called *Mysteries of the Unexplained*. It is aimed at young teenagers. Your job is to write the opening double-page spread to grab your readers' interest and make them want to read on. You should cover a range of topics, for example, hauntings, vampires, zombies. You mustn't write anything that is bloodthirsty or will upset anyone. You could include:

- a definition of the words *vampire* and *zombie*
- an example of each from history, with comments from experts explaining what they might really have been or what might really have happened.

Think about:

- how you will set out your pages
- which information you will include
- what tone of voice you will use (for example, serious or humorous)
- how you will present the information – using text, images, headings, bullet points, magazine logos, tables, and so on.

Funny ha ha

Starting points

Different people find different things funny. Some people love physical humour. They like comedy in which people trip on banana skins or fall through doors. Other people find it childish. They prefer verbal humour – jokes based on what people say, rather than what they do.

What makes you laugh? In pairs or in small groups talk about films, books, television shows and comedians that you find funny. Then talk about some that you don't find funny at all. Do you all agree with each other? Create a top five funny and unfunny list to compare with others in your class.

Comedians talking

People sometimes say that beneath the surface comedians are often worried, unhappy or lonely. What is it like to earn a living as a comedian and how did some comics start?

Here a number of professional comics look back to their early days …

DOMINIC HOLLAND

I've always loved comedy, I've always loved making people laugh. It's the only thing I've ever done well. I've done everything OK. I've been OK at school, OK at football. But comedy has always been my thing. People have always said, 'Dominic, you're funny – you should be a comedian.' I've been doing it since I was a kid.

MARK LAMARR

Pre-school is the time for laughter. Not only have you got no cares or worries in the world, you've got no problems with what you laugh at, at all. Sean Lock told me about these three- and four-year-old kids he saw when he was round at someone's house. One of them came in with her mum's hat on and they all wrapped themselves up in a sleeping bag and laughed for half an hour. Every time they looked up at each other they died laughing. You have much more fun then than you do at school.

JENNY ECLAIR

I had an idyllic childhood. This is why I've had problems. When I've had therapy, people have always delved into my childhood and said, 'Well, there must have been something wrong?' And I've said, 'No. Actually, nothing has quite lived up to it since – that's been the problem.' I was very happy as a child. I had a mad time, I had a right laugh. I loved my teenage years as well – there were some miserable times, but I always had loads of boyfriends. I had a great time. Schoolwork was easy enough for me to get by. It's the responsibilities of being an adult – I don't actually like being an adult very much.

STEVE COOGAN

One of my warmest family memories was watching *Fawlty Towers*. It really was a family event, because we loved comedy. It was a Catholic family, and we didn't like crude comedy – we liked inventive, intelligent comedy. My dad used to play Hancock tapes to me, and the Goons. I remember the whole family being called down, all eight of us, and the whole family would congregate in the living room. There were eight people in the room, laughing, watching the TV. And afterwards, we'd turn the TV off and my mum would be exhausted. With tears of laughter in her eyes, she'd say, 'Put the kettle on! Let's sit down and have a cup of tea to recover from it!' It was a real event.

Activities

1 Mark Lamarr says 'You have much more fun then [at three or four] than you do at school.' In pairs or in a small group, spend five minutes thinking back to your earliest memories. You might focus on:

- memories of your family
- going to nursery school
- first friends
- birthday parties or outings.

Did life seem different then? Did it seem more fun? Each try to think of a funny incident that took place before you were aged five.

2 Steve Coogan remembers his whole family enjoying *Fawlty Towers*. Try to imagine yourself in the future, about fifteen years from now. What current comedy show might you remember well? Try to explain why.

3 Dominic Holland learned early on that he was naturally comic. Think of anyone you know who is a natural comedian. Try to describe what it is about them that makes them amusing. Is it:

- their looks?
- the way they speak?
- the things they say?
- the way they behave?

Try to think of a specific example of something this person has said or done which showed they were funny.

4 What do you think Jenny Eclair means when she says she had 'an idyllic childhood. This is why I've had problems'?

Writing comedy

A situation comedy is a television comedy show usually set in one situation or context. For example, the situation in *Fawlty Towers* is a hotel run by a married couple who are always arguing.

These are notes issued on the Internet by the BBC Comedy Department, giving advice to new writers on how to write a successful sitcom.

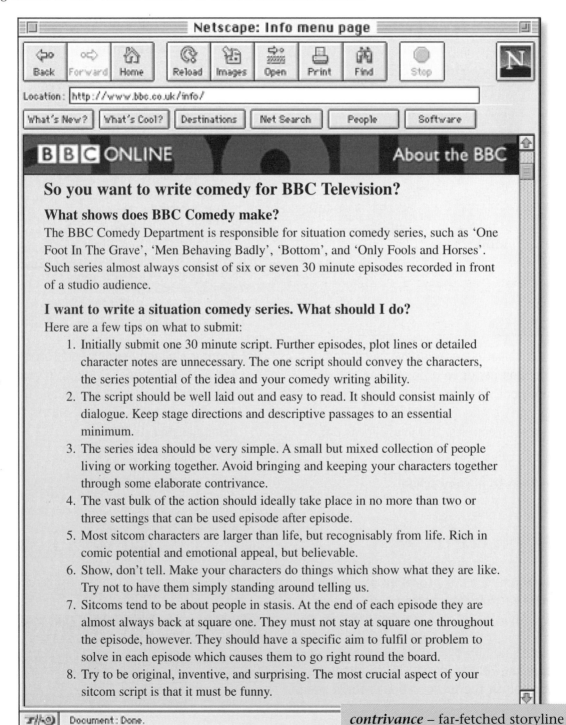

Netscape: Info menu page

Back | Forward | Home | Reload | Images | Open | Print | Find | Stop

Location: http://www.bbc.co.uk/info/

What's New? | What's Cool? | Destinations | Net Search | People | Software

BBC ONLINE — About the BBC

So you want to write comedy for BBC Television?

What shows does BBC Comedy make?

The BBC Comedy Department is responsible for situation comedy series, such as 'One Foot In The Grave', 'Men Behaving Badly', 'Bottom', and 'Only Fools and Horses'. Such series almost always consist of six or seven 30 minute episodes recorded in front of a studio audience.

I want to write a situation comedy series. What should I do?

Here are a few tips on what to submit:

1. Initially submit one 30 minute script. Further episodes, plot lines or detailed character notes are unnecessary. The one script should convey the characters, the series potential of the idea and your comedy writing ability.
2. The script should be well laid out and easy to read. It should consist mainly of dialogue. Keep stage directions and descriptive passages to an essential minimum.
3. The series idea should be very simple. A small but mixed collection of people living or working together. Avoid bringing and keeping your characters together through some elaborate contrivance.
4. The vast bulk of the action should ideally take place in no more than two or three settings that can be used episode after episode.
5. Most sitcom characters are larger than life, but recognisably from life. Rich in comic potential and emotional appeal, but believable.
6. Show, don't tell. Make your characters do things which show what they are like. Try not to have them simply standing around telling us.
7. Sitcoms tend to be about people in stasis. At the end of each episode they are almost always back at square one. They must not stay at square one throughout the episode, however. They should have a specific aim to fulfil or problem to solve in each episode which causes them to go right round the board.
8. Try to be original, inventive, and surprising. The most crucial aspect of your sitcom script is that it must be funny.

Document: Done.

contrivance – far-fetched storyline
in stasis – who never change

Activities

1 Most of the advice is about characters. Look at the main points listed below and try to think of a character from a situation comedy who fits the description. Think of comedies like: *The Vicar of Dibley, Men Behaving Badly, Fawlty Towers, Dad's Army, The Brittas Empire, Blackadder, One Foot in the Grave*.

Character	Example
A small but mixed group of people living or working together	
Larger than life but believable	
People in stasis – they haven't really changed by the end of each episode	

Can you think of any sitcom characters who break any of these rules?

2 Working in pairs or in a small group, use the comedy advice to develop your own sitcom outline. Spend twenty to thirty minutes brainstorming ideas about settings and characters. Think of some possible storylines. Then make a presentation of your idea to the rest of the class.

Think about:

Setting

● somewhere that brings a mixed group of people together, for example a hotel or a leisure centre

● somewhere simple enough not to need many scene changes

● somewhere that will be familiar to the audience.

Characters

● quirky characters, but who feel real – otherwise we won't believe in the show

● people with different personalities, so that there is room for conflict

● people who do things rather than just stand around telling jokes

● a central character who wants to achieve something and probably fails.

3 How useful do you find the BBC advice on writing comedy? Would it help you to write a show of your own? Do you have any questions which it leaves unanswered?

Basil the Rat

Look more closely at the way situation comedy works by reading aloud the following classic example taken from *Fawlty Towers*. One person should be the narrator to read the stage directions in italics.

The story so far ...

Manuel's pet rat is on the loose in the hotel on the very day that Mr Carnegie, a health inspector, has arrived. The staff are desperately looking for the rat (called Basil), whilst pretending to Basil Fawlty that there's nothing wrong ...

CAST

Basil Fawlty – hotel manager
Sybil – Basil's wife
Terry – the chef
Manuel – the waiter
Polly – the waitress
Carnegie – the health inspector

BASIL *strides out of the bar and goes into the kitchen, where* TERRY *is looking behind the fridge which he has pulled out from the wall.*

TERRY I'm just cleaning behind the fridge, Mr Fawlty.

BASIL *looks at him and pushes the dining-room door open. He looks in, comes out, checks, and goes back in. In the dining room,* POLLY *is kneeling under a table, only her rear and legs visible.* BASIL *walks quietly up behind her.*

POLLY Basil ... Basil ... cheesies ... Basil ...

BASIL Yes? *(there is a thump and the table jerks upwards,* POLLY *appears)* Here I am!

POLLY Oh, hallo, Mr Fawlty ...

BASIL Oh, that's for me, is it? Thank you.

POLLY Oh ... *(he takes the piece of cheese from her hand and eats it)* Shall I get you some more, there's plenty ...

BASIL He's called Basil, is he? ... Don't play dumb with me, I trusted you, you're responsible for this. 'Oh, I've got a friend who'll look after him, Mr Fawlty'! *(he is about to hit her when he sees* MANUEL *crawling out from under another table;* BASIL *runs after him and* MANUEL *scuttles back under the table)* Come on. Come on out, come on, Basil's here. *(he makes kiss-kiss noises)*

TERRY   *(coming in from the kitchen)* Have you got him?

BASIL   … He's under there.

TERRY   Right. I'll get him. *(he goes towards the table and then stops, rather sheepish)*

BASIL   Cleaning behind the fridge, hmm?

TERRY   Well, we didn't want to worry you, you've got a lot on your mind Mr Fawlty.

BASIL   What, you mean a Public Health Inspector coming after a twenty-four-hour warning and a rat loose in the hotel, is that what you mean?

POLLY   He must have escaped, Mr Fawlty, and come back …

BASIL   Come **back**?

POLLY   *(desperately)* They home.

BASIL   Oh, I see, he's a **homing** rat, is he?

TERRY   … Oh yeah, rats are amazing creatures, Mr Fawlty. I read about one once, his owner had gone down to Penzance …

BASIL   Yes, yes, I read about that. When the chef got filleted with his own carving knife …

TERRY   No, honest, Mr Fawlty, scout's honour.

POLLY   We'll find him, Mr Fawlty!

BASIL   Well, if you could, that would be lovely. Before they close us down. Super. Well, let's have a little Basil hunt, shall we, and then we'll deal with the sackings later.

TERRY   I'll do the cellar.

POLLY   I'll do this floor. Manuel, you check your room.

BASIL   Start in the bar, Polly, it was there two minutes ago. I'll do the kitchen. *(he goes into the kitchen and starts checking the cupboards)*

TERRY   I've done all them. *(he goes out of the back door)*

BASIL *remembers another cupboard, goes and gets rat poison from it, then runs to the fridge where he finds a plate of veal fillets. He takes one, sprinkles some poison on it, puts it on the floor, leaves the poison on top of the fridge and washes his hands. He goes into the lobby, and goes behind the reception desk.* MR CARNEGIE *comes in and* SYBIL, *coming down the stairs, greets him.*

SYBIL   Oh, Mr Carnegie. Good morning.

CARNEGIE   Good morning, Mrs Fawlty.

BASIL   Oh, hallo. Nice to see you.

SYBIL   Would you like some coffee before we adjourn to …

CARNEGIE   No thank you. If we start upstairs with the water tanks …

BASIL   Ah, good idea.

CARNEGIE   What?

BASIL   Good thinking. About starting upstairs. Sybil, would you like to show Mr Carnegie upstairs?

SYBIL   I was just going to, Basil.

BASIL   Yes, and I'll keep an eye on things down here, shall I, see if I can find something to be getting on with …

The gun goes off in the bar. They all jump.

CARNEGIE   Good God, what was that?

BASIL   Bloody television exploding again. I'll deal with it. You go upstairs. *(he hurries towards the bar)*

CARNEGIE   That was a gun!

SYBIL   Yes, it did sound like it, didn't it.

POLLY *runs in carrying a large net. She sees* MR CARNEGIE; *he sees her.*

POLLY   Moths.

Activities

1 Focus on the character of Basil Fawlty. Based on the scene you have just read, write down some words to describe his personality. Try to think of six different words. Use a spider diagram like the one below:

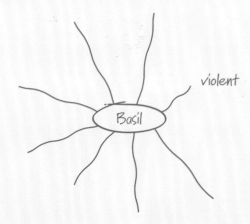

2 Look at the list below. It gives some of the ingredients which make the scene funny. In pairs, decide which is the most important and which is the least important ingredient:

1 The rat has the same name as Mr Fawlty.

2 Polly bangs her head on the table.

3 Basil Fawlty pretends at first that he doesn't know the others are looking for a rat.

4 Basil is extremely sarcastic.

5 Basil changes his tone as soon as Mr Carnegie arrives – he suddenly becomes very polite.

6 Sybil is very calm, in contrast to Basil.

7 The gun goes off, startling everyone.

8 Polly pretends to be catching moths.

Bean: The Ultimate Disaster Movie

In 1997 Rowan Atkinson and writer Richard Curtis made the popular television show *Mr Bean* into a feature film.

The story so far ...

Mr Bean has been mistaken for a world art expert and invited to the USA. In fact, he's an art gallery attendant. He is to stay at the home of the Langley household – where Mrs Langley, in particular, is not looking forward to meeting him. Little does she know that he is already inside the house ...

CAST

Mr Bean
David Langley – father
Alison Langley – mother
Kevin and Jennifer – their two children

Ext. = exterior scene
Int. = interior scene

Ext. The Langley house – Night

The taxi draws up outside the house. Mr Bean *gets out with his case. Sees the letter box, with the number 1150 on it. Checks his slip of paper. Yup – this is the place. He walks up to the front door and presses the doorbell. No answer. Presses again. Still no answer ... Now where have they hidden the key? He inspects things carefully.*

The camera sees what he sees ... the doormat, the flowerpots, the window ledge ... and then he spots a little stone frog. Mr Bean *smiles. Key-hiding is something he knows about – and people are pathetically obvious about it.* Mr Bean *picks up the frog to reveal the key. It glints in the porch light.*

Int. The Langley house. Hallway – Night

Mr Bean *lets himself in. The house is dark.*

Mr Bean   Anybody at home?

Ext. The Langley house – Night

Alison's *car draws up outside. The* Langleys *have arrived home.*

Int. The Langley house. Kitchen/Living room/Landing – Night

The exhausted family enter an apparently untouched, dark house.

DAVID   Right. I'll check the machine. He might have left a message.

ALISON   He might have missed the plane. That'd be good.

Int. The Langley house. David and Alison's bedroom – Night

It's a little later. DAVID *enters the bedroom.* ALISON *is sitting on the bed, TV switched on, exhausted …* DAVID *starts to undress.*

DAVID   Well – there's no message.

Int. The Langley house. Bathroom – Night

MR BEAN, *in his pyjamas, is just finishing washing his socks in the sink. The water is filthy. He hums along happily to music on a Walkman.*

Int. The Langley house. David and Alison's bedroom – Night

DAVID   Oh, he'll be fine. I mean, don't you think?

ALISON   *(watching TV)* David – I've never met the guy. I don't want to meet the guy. If he never sets foot in this house, that's just fine by me.

Int. The Langley house. Landing – Night

MR BEAN, *still humming, wrings out his socks and exits to the landing.*

Int. The Langley house. Landing – Night

MR BEAN *heads for a bedroom. As the door quietly closes we see the sign on the door: 'Jennifer'. The doors on this landing all do look dangerously similar.*

Ext. The Langley house – Day

The next morning. Shot from across the street. A newspaper boy delivers. Birds sing. It's a lovely, peaceful, early morning. A long scream comes from the house.

Int. The Langley house. Upstairs landing – Day

JENNIFER *hurtles out of her room screaming. She runs and locks herself in the bathroom. The rest of the family run out on to the landing.*

ALISON   What is it? Jennifer!

JENNIFER *(V/O)*   … there's a man …

DAVID   Honey, calm down … it's OK.

JENNIFER *(V/O)*   There's a man. I woke up next to a man …

DAVID   It's OK. There's no one out here. It's just a nightmare.

Pause … then a click of the bathroom lock … JENNIFER *comes out. Then there's another click.* MR BEAN *breezes out of* JENNIFER'S *bedroom, past the family, in his pyjamas, carrying a washbag and a towel over his arm.*

MR BEAN   *(airily)* Morning.

He waves to them friendlily, slips into the bathroom and closes the door.

The family stare in amazement.

Int. The Langley house. Living room – Day

Simple shot of MR BEAN, *sitting alone in the middle of the big couch. Opposite sit the entire family on the other couch – echoes of the scene when* DAVID *asked the kids what they thought of the idea of* MR BEAN *coming.*

DAVID   So … ahm … Doctor …

MR BEAN *misinterprets* DAVID'S *nervous hesitation as ignorance of his name.*

MR BEAN   Bean.

DAVID   Yes – so, Dr Bean …

Worried look from MR BEAN – *what's he talking about?*

DAVID   … you made it. *(*MR BEAN *nods)* Nice flight? *(*MR BEAN *nods)* This is Kevin. *(*MR BEAN *nods)* This is Jennifer. *(*MR BEAN *nods)* And this is my wife Alison. *(*MR BEAN *nods again)*

ALISON   David? Could I just have the tiniest talk with you in the kitchen?

Int. The Langley house. Kitchen – Day

DAVID   I appreciate on first viewing, he's eccentric.

ALISON   David, there are Martians who have been exiled from Mars for looking weird who look less weird than this guy.

DAVID   Yes, he has an original quality about him. But I'm sure in time …

ALISON   He goes today.

Int. The Langley house. Living room – Day

MR BEAN *takes an M&M from a large glass bowl of them on the table, throws it high in the air and catches it in his mouth.*

KEVIN   Pretty cool. Can you do this?

He pulls an exceptionally weird face. MR BEAN *likes it.*

MR BEAN   No. But I can do this.

He wiggles his ears. KEVIN *loves it.*

KEVIN   Neat, wow … how do you do that?

MR BEAN   Magic.

Int. The Langley house. Kitchen – Day

ALISON *has won the argument.*

ALISON   So you'll say something today?

DAVID   Yes, OK. Today sounds like a good day.

At which moment, MR BEAN *enters. He crosses the kitchen and removes his dried underpants from the oven. This does not strengthen* DAVID's *position.*

Ext. David's car – Day

DAVID *is chatting away eagerly. He has not yet realised the extent to which* MR BEAN *is not 'Dr Bean'.*

DAVID Well, sir, an unorthodox start – but I never expected things with a man of your calibre to be normal. You certainly … made an impression on Alison: she was a little thrown this morning – but, believe me, when you get to know her – she's the most wonderful woman in the United States. You married, Doctor?

MR BEAN *laughs and shakes his head.*

DAVID Like to play the field, eh?

MR BEAN *laughs again – but when* DAVID *turns to him he has become serious.*

MR BEAN I beg your pardon …

DAVID No, no, I'm sure a man like you has … dedicated his life to his work. I hate to confess, I haven't actually read anything of yours. Tell me, Doctor, what exactly is your position at the gallery?

MR BEAN I sit in the corner and look at the paintings.

DAVID Brilliant. Perfect! If only more scholars would do that. Just sit and look. Not lecture, not write, not argue – just sit and look at the paintings themselves.

MR BEAN *is puzzled by this.*

Activities

1 Start by discussing the character of Mr Bean based on the screenplay you have just read. Look at the comments below of some viewers and decide which you agree and disagree with:

- Mr Bean is hilarious because he gets so many things wrong.
- There's something quite sad about the character of Mr Bean.
- Mr Bean is a lonely person.
- Mr Bean is quite a disturbing character.
- The film encourages us to laugh at people who don't fit in to society.
- Mr Bean isn't funny.

2 Which parts of the screenplay did you find most and least funny? Try to think of other jokes which could have taken place in the Langley scene.

3 Compare the way Alison (the mother) and Kevin (the son) react to Mr Bean. She finds him 'weird'; he thinks he's 'neat'. Imagine what each would say in a letter to a friend about their new visitor. Don't write the whole letter – just a paragraph or two from each. Use each paragraph to show what they feel about Mr Bean, giving as many specific examples from the screenplay as possible. You might start like this:

Kevin

Dear Joe
We've got this great new visitor staying...

Alison

Dear Saskia
You're not going to believe what's going on here...

Mr Bean: the critics

When *Bean: The Ultimate Disaster Movie* was released in the UK, it received a mixed reception. It did well at the box office, selling plenty of tickets. But the newspaper critics were mostly negative about the film. Compare these two reviews:

Bean fan: Barney   Picture: Karen Fuchs

BEAN: THE ULTIMATE DISASTER MOVIE

Even the title sounds a little unsure of itself. Since when did movies go around actually calling themselves movies, unless they needed urgent reassurance of the fact? *Bean: The Ultimate Disaster Movie* is certainly a brave attempt to enlarge the small, grub-like comedy of ITV's *Mr Bean* to fill a feature film, but even the highly rubberised talents of Rowan Atkinson look sorely overstretched: try as he might, Bean keeps pinging back to the dimensions of the small screen.

The biggest thing about it, I suppose, is the fact that Bean has acquired an extra edge of pathos and, for the first time, been made to talk, which surely defeats the point of the guy – a little like asking Eddie Murphy to keep it quiet.

I have enough problems as it is with any silent comedy made after the advent of the talkies, but silent comedy that doesn't stay silent: who is that going to please, exactly?

The script, by Richard Curtis, has Mr Bean mistaken for an eminent art historian, and flown over to oversee the hand over of Whistler's painting of his mother to a Californian art gallery, where he must deliver the keynote speech. 'Try to keep it under one hour,' Bean is told, 'and it would be good if you could put a joke in it.' They should have told that to Curtis: the movie revolves around a single joke, but it's way over an hour.

TOM SHONE

A young critic gives his verdict

WHEN Rowan Atkinson is playing the role of Mr Bean, he likes to imagine himself as a nine-year-old boy. So who better to judge the disaster-prone twit's first full-length film than my son Barney, aged not-quite-10?

As a veteran *Bean*-watcher, Barney is well acquainted with the programme. It appeals to children because, like them, Bean is a mix of innocence and guile. They recognise his awkwardness – the world, after all, is a frightening place – while applauding his cunning strategies.

Bean the film is less inventive than its television version, though Bean himself is more fleshed out. He even speaks quite a lot. Does the boy with a ready laugh approve of these changes? 'Brilliant. Can we get the video when it comes out?'

But he wasn't laughing nearly as much as he does at home. And in the first five minutes the film had repeated a couple of gags from the television shows. 'That's all right. In fact, it was better because this time when he burst the sickbag on the plane you got to see the vomit.'

Barney is a vulgarian who can usually be found teaching his younger brothers to burp in time to a song. As a fan of *Bottom*, *Men Behaving Badly* and *The Fast Show*'s cruder bits, surely he found *Bean's* silent slapstick a bit tame? After all, there's no swearing and hardly any jokes about bodily functions. 'I like all kinds of humour, Dad, some childish, some grown-up.'

Well, excuse me. But if this young person of eclectic taste does not identify with the nine-year-old child inside Mr Bean, who is he reminded of when watching the rubber-faced loon? 'He's more like you, Dad – a bit of a prat, really, only funnier.'

ALISTAIR FRASER

vulgarian – someone with common tastes
pathos – emotion
eminent – well-known
of eclectic taste – liking a variety of styles

Activities

1 To help you to compare the two reviews in detail, copy out the checklist below and place a tick in the appropriate boxes.

Question	Review A	Review B
1 Which review is more positive about the character of Mr Bean?		
2 Which review gives a better idea of what the film is actually like?		
3 Which review is easier to follow?		
4 Which review seems more fair?		
5 Which review did you prefer?		

2 Now discuss the reasons for your choices, using examples from the two reviews as much as possible.

ASSIGNMENTS

1 Comedians talking

What makes people in your class laugh? Which TV comedy programmes and films do people find the most funny? How do these compare with the views of your parents? Does your 'top ten' list of comedy shows look very different from an adult one?

Devise a questionnaire and do some research to find out about the comedy tastes of different generations.

Present your findings in a report.

2 Sitcom

Think back to the work you did on situation comedy on page 77. Either using the ideas developed in your group, or starting again on your own, write the opening pages of a script for a new comedy show. Think of:

- a title
- the main characters
- the setting
- what will happen in the opening episode.

Write the first scene, referring back to the BBC comedy advice on page 76. To help you with the layout of your script, look at the screenplays of *Fawlty Towers* or *Mr Bean*.

3 Critics

Choose a comedy film or programme you really like. Write a newspaper review of it. Remember that you are trying to:

- entertain your readers – so make your writing lively and fun
- give your readers a flavour of what the show is like – so give examples
- judge the show – so be critical, saying what is successful and unsuccessful.

To make your review as real as possible, aim to write exactly 500 words.

Campaign!

Passive smoking

The leaflet on pages 90–91 is designed to warn people about the dangers of passive smoking. Recent research has shown that passive smoking can have a damaging effect on your health even if you never smoke a cigarette yourself. Look at how this leaflet presents the case against passive smoking and then work through the following activities.

Activities

1 Test your understanding of the leaflet by answering the following questions.

   1 What percentage of the smoker's smoke is breathed in by the smoker?

   2 How many chemicals in tobacco smoke can cause cancer?

   3 Name three effects passive smoking can have on children and babies.

   4 How does Britain's approach to passive smoking differ from that of other countries?

Activities

2 Look at the design of the leaflet. Do you think the design features it uses are effective? Try to explain your opinion. Use a table like the one below to help you.

Feature	Is effective	Is not effective	Comment
Question and Answer (Q&A) format			
Facts and figures giving the source of the information			
Photograph of a baby s bowl with food in one side and cigarette stubs in the other			
Bullet points to give quick information and advice			

3 How successful do you think the leaflet is in warning readers about the dangers of passive smoking?

In pairs or in small groups, decide how you would improve the leaflet. What would you change about:

● the layout?

● the language (for example, length of sentences and vocabulary)?

● the use of facts and statistics?

On a large sheet of paper, produce some sample designs and sample sentences to show the changes you would make. Present these to another group, or to the rest of your class.

Q A What is passive smoking?

Passive smoking is breathing in other people's tobacco smoke. Other people's tobacco smoke is sometimes called environmental tobacco smoke.

Q A Why should I be worried?

Only 15 per cent of the smoke from a cigarette is inhaled by the smoker – the rest goes into the surrounding air and other people can breathe it in.

Breathing air which contains tobacco smoke can be bad for your health. This is because the tiny particles and gases in tobacco smoke contain over 4000 chemicals, many of which are harmful – at least 60 are known to cause cancer. The gases also include carbon monoxide, the poisonous gas that comes out of car exhausts.

15%

Q A What is the effect on my health?

Breathing other people's smoke is uncomfortable and can cause

- ✖ nose, throat and chest irritation and breathing difficulties
- ✖ coughing
- ✖ sneezing
- ✖ red and running eyes
- ✖ a runny nose
- ✖ headaches
- ✖ dizziness
- ✖ nausea and lack of concentration.

If you have a long-term health problem, such as asthma, chronic bronchitis or certain allergies, passive smoking can make it worse.

Doctors now say that passive smoking causes serious and sometimes fatal illnesses. The UK Government's Independent

2

Q A What's in cigarette smoke?

Carbon monoxide – the same gas that comes out of car exhausts – is the main gas in cigarette smoke. The smoke also contains over 4000 other chemicals. Some of these have links with cancer in humans – arsenic, benzene, chromium, nickel, vinyl chloride, cadmium, formaldehyde etc. The complete list begins:

85%

carbon monoxide, nicotine, nitrogen oxides, 2-nitropropane, hydrogen cyanide, ammonia, dimethyl-amine, 2.5-dimethylamine, ethylamine, methyl-amine, methylpyrazines, 2-,3-, and 4-methylpyr-idines, 1-methylpyrrolidine, pyridine, pyrrolidine, trimethylamine, hydrazine, acetal- dehyde, acetone

based on Tobacco or Health? Smoke-free Europe 4 , WHO.

Scientific Committee on Smoking and Health has estimated that several hundred non-smokers die each year from lung cancer caused by passive smoking. The risk of lung cancer from passive smoking is small, but some 50 to 100 times greater than the risk of lung cancer from exposure to asbestos.

Also, passive smoking may be linked to heart disease and death from heart attack.

passive smoking can increase the risk of lung cancer by between 10 and 30 per cent

based on the Fourth Report of the Independent Scientific Committee on Smoking & Health, 1988

3

Q What's the effect on children's health?

A

Babies and children who cannot avoid smoke where they
live and play are at
particular risk. Babies of
smokers are much more
likely to be taken to hospital with
chest trouble in their first year of life
than non-smokers' children.

Children with a parent who smokes
have more chest, ear, nose and throat
infections than non-smokers' children.
And the more cigarettes smoked at
home, the greater the risk to the child.
Children exposed to smoke are more
likely to develop breathing problems as adults.

Unborn babies are also at risk from passive smoking.

The risk to unborn babies of pregnant women who smoke has been
known for many years, but it now seems that unborn babies of
pregnant non-smoking women are also at risk if
the women are exposed to passive smoking.

Women who have been regularly exposed to
passive smoking during pregnancy tend to have
smaller babies. Being small at birth makes it
harder for the baby to make a good start in life.

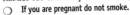

the risk of having an underweight baby can be increased by passive smoking

○ If you are pregnant do not smoke.
○ Avoid smoky places.
○ Family and friends should avoid smoking in front
  of children and pregnant women. Ask your guests
  not to smoke.

4

Q What can I do to clear the air?

A

European countries
with completely or
partially smoke-free
buses and trains ▽

The trouble with tobacco smoke is that
it gets everywhere. Separating smokers
and non-smokers in the same room
may reduce the level of smoke in the
non-smoking area, but this is not enough.

Air filters, ventilators or extraction systems
may reduce, but do not prevent,
exposure to other people's smoke.

We must make sure that
non-smokers do not have to live or
work in smoky conditions by ensuring
that all enclosed public places
are smoke-free. Where
appropriate, separate rooms
should be provided for
smoking.

based on World Health Organisation figures

Although many countries in Europe and elsewhere now have laws
to ensure that smoking is restricted in public places, the British
Government has taken a different approach so far. It encourages
restrictions on smoking in public places. But in practice it is

mainly left to
employers and those
who control public
buildings and
transport to decide
whether or not
smoking should be
restricted.

THE PERCENTAGE OF
SMOKE-FREE PUBLIC
PLACES WORLDWIDE

schools & colleges 33%
places of entertainment 33%
health services 40%
public places over 50% based on World Health Organisation figures

5

GASP Protest

The following text is the transcript of a television news broadcast from the USA. It describes how an organization called GASP (Group Against Smoking Pollution) launched a campaign for a non-smoking airport.

TRANSCRIPT:

The following transcript and video clips are of a
CBS-affiliate Channel 4 News segment broadcast
Saturday, July 13, 1996, at around 6:00 pm

CONNORS: The question of public smoking is sparking some new controversy in St. Louis.

HUNTER: At issue this time: Should Lambert International be smoke-free? Wendy Roylance shows us some protesters choosing a rather dramatic way of voicing their opinions.

ROYLANCE: *[off camera]* These white jump suits and masks look like something you'd see at a dioxin cleanup site. Instead, anti-smoking protesters are wearing them in front of St. Louis City Hall.

[Shot of GASP protesters on sidewalk outside city hall holding placards. Closeup of Pion wearing suit and respirator. Closeup of sign on back of protester with GASP logo and words "Smoke Busters."]

They want Lambert International Airport smoke-free.

[Shot of smoker sitting in airport in front of sign reading "Smoking Area".]

PION: *[in interview with Roylance while holding respirator down to uncover mouth]*
I wear this in an airport, I've worn this in an airport. It's got a HEPA filter for taking out particulates, and its got a, an activated charcoal filter for taking out gases, but it doesn't, it's not a 100%. A lot of it still gets through.

ROYLANCE: *[off camera]* Right now, open smoking is allowed in 7 areas of the airport, but protesters say there should be no smoking anywhere.
[Shot of wall sign showing location of designated smoking areas in each terminal level headed SMOKING PERMITTED IN DESIGNATED SMOKING AREAS; shot of smokers smoking in designated smoking area.]

McCANDLISS: *[in interview with Roylance]*
Many, many buildings are now smoke-free. It can be done and, er, er and I think the airport should do it.

ROYLANCE: *[moving to stand in front of "Smoking Area" sign in airport]*
Lambert airport officials tell News 4 there are no plans to make the airport smoke-free, but they are considering adding smoking lounges to isolate the smokers. *[Shot of Steve Newman standing in concourse.]* Smoker Steve Newman says he shouldn't have to go to a smoking lounge to smoke.

NEWMAN: *[in interview with Roylance while standing in airport concourse]*
It ain't really right, but I, I can respect someone that don't want to smell it, but they oughta respect somebody that does want to have one too.

ROYLANCE: *[shot of Roylance with back to camera seated next to Delmas]*
Shirley Delmas says she would use a smoking lounge only if she has to.

DELMAS: *[in interview seated next to Roylance, then in closeup]*
If the smoking lounges would be, er, close to each concourse, er, I think that might work all right and that would satisfy everybody.

ROYLANCE: *[off camera]*
Seven smoking lounges will be built at the airport by November. *[smoker shown lighting up, followed by shot of baggage]* Protesters say that's still not right. They say they won't stop until Lambert Airport is smoke-free.

[Shot of Pion holding respirator, followed by closeup of GASP banner draped over seat in front of city hall.]

McCANDLISS: *[in interview with Roylance]*
I would like to think that St. Louis would be up to that kind of progress, yes.

ROYLANCE: *[off camera, over closeup of Delmas lighting cigarette in designated smoking area]*
At Lambert Airport, Wendy Roylance, News 4.

HUNTER: The Missouri Group Against Smoking Pollution plans to present an airport smoking petition to St. Louis City officials in the near future.

Activities

1 Working in small groups, read the text of the broadcast aloud. Each group will need people to play the following roles:

Larry Connors – news anchor (news presenter)
Julius Hunter – news anchor
Wendy Roylance – local reporter
Martin Pion – president of Missouri GASP
Candy McCandliss – GASP supporter
Steve Newman and **Shirley Delmas** – two smokers interviewed at the airport.

Spend some time in your groups rehearsing the news report so that it feels real. When your group is ready, perform it to another group. Then watch their report.

Both groups had the same script: how do the reports differ? Try to discuss any differences in detail – for example, the way people sit or stand; the way they say the words; the speed of delivery, and so on.

2 What do you think of the GASP campaign? Do you think it is likely to succeed in making the airport authorities change their approach? Does it just feel like a cheap publicity stunt?

3 Imagine that a GASP campaigner and someone from Lambert-St Louis airport agree to be interviewed on a news programme. The presenter asks them their opinions. What will happen? Improvise or script a discussion about whether the airport should be smoke-free.

Charity advertisements

Newspapers often carry advertisements for charities. As people tend to skim newspapers quite quickly, looking for stories that interest them, these advertisements have to grab the reader's attention. Sometimes their style can be almost shocking. Look at the two examples which follow and decide if you think they are successful.

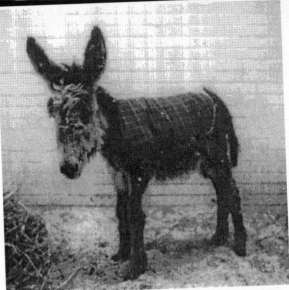

SHAKING WITH FEAR, HER MOTHER GONE, this little donkey was in a desperate situation. If we had not been there to save her - Flora would have been cruelly **PUT TO DEATH**.

Every day our teams help donkeys in distress around the world.

WE NEED YOUR SUPPORT - PLEASE SEND ANY DONATION NO MATTER HOW SMALL. Thank you.

Please note our administration and fund raising costs are only 8.4p in the £1.

Please send donations to:
The International Donkey Protection Trust,
(Dept   ), Sidmouth,
Devon, EX10 0NU.
Tel: (01395) 578222
Enquiries to Dr E. D. Svendsen, M.B.E.

Reg. Charity No. 271410

I enclose Cheque/Postal Order for £ _____
Name: Mr/Mrs/Miss _____
Address _____

Why bother? She'll probably die anyway

It's true her chances of survival are less than children in this country – but it's not hopeless.

If you sponsor a child like Thani through ACTIONAID, you'll not only improve her chances of survival, but you'll also give her a better opportunity in life. By working closely with the child's community, we can provide access to safe water, health care, education, agricultural training and a means of earning their own living.

In return for your support, you'll receive a photo and messages from the child you sponsor. And you'll always know exactly how your money is helping through regular project reports from our field workers.

Sponsoring a child really can help change the future. So why not do it today?

☐ Please send me details about sponsoring a child, or call: **01460 61073.**
I am interested in sponsoring in:
☐Africa   ☐Asia   ☐Where there's greatest need.
☐ I can't sponsor a child now, but enclose a gift of:
☐£200   ☐£100   ☐£50   ☐£25   ☐£_____
Make cheques/POs payable to ACTIONAID, and send to: ACTIONAID, FREEPOST BS4868, Chard, Somerset TA20 1BR.

Mr/Mrs/Miss/Ms _____

Address _____
_____
_____

Postcode _____
Tel. _____

ACTIONAID™
A registered charity No. 274467

Activities

1 Look more closely at the two advertisements and decide:

- which one seems more emotional
- which one seems easier to understand
- which one has the more eye-catching headline
- which one would make you want to support the charity.

Give reasons to support your opinions. In pairs or in small groups, compare your reactions to the two texts.

2 The advertisement for the Donkey Sanctuary encourages us to pity the donkey in the photograph. How does it do this?

3 Choose an issue or topic you feel strongly about, such as vegetarianism, cruelty to animals, or a disease you know about. Design a newspaper advertisement to encourage people to support your cause. Try to:

- think of a good name for your made-up charity
- design a logo
- think of a headline
- think of a photograph you could use to add impact
- write the text, keeping paragraphs and sentences short.

Selling on air

Roger Pett is an advertising copywriter. He writes campaigns and commercials for magazines, television and radio. He wrote the following two commercials for Vista Vacations. The company wanted people to know about the range of holidays they offered, and they wanted to use the tag-line 'We've got it all, so you've got it made'. The rest was up to the writer.

Practise reading them aloud, making them sound as professional as possible. The first commercial is designed to last 30 seconds, the second to last 40 seconds.

> **tag-line** – slogan, a phrase which is simple and easy to remember
> **SVO** – single voice over
> **SFX** – sound effects

Vista Vacations   30 sec Radio Commercial   Title: The brochure

SVO	'If you like ...'
SFX	Flamenco Music
SVO	'Or you may prefer ...'
SFX	Sounds of Bazaar with Middle eastern music
SVO	'Or perhaps you have an inclination for ...'
SFX	Waves on the beach — sea birds calling
SVO	'What ever type of holiday suits you best, call free today on 0890 1234 and order your new Vista Vacations brochure. That's 0890 1234. Vista Vacations. We've got it all, so you've got it made.'

Vista Vacations   40 sec Radio Commercial   Title: Holiday choice

SFX   Surf on the beach. Caribbean music in background.
SVO   'You've worked hard for your holiday, so it has to be right.

        You need to know that the holiday that you have booked is the holiday that you want. And that the accommodation has been thoroughly vetted to meet the most exacting industry standards.

        Book your holiday with Vista Vacations and that's just what you get.

        In fact we offer a wider range of holidays than anyone else in the business.

        We've got family holidays, activity holidays, quiet relaxing holidays. And we've got week-end breaks.

        And all at prices that you will enjoy.

        So, if you are looking for a holiday package that won't cost a packet, call for your free brochure on 0890 1234.

        That's 0890 1234.

        Even the call is free.

        Vista Vacations. We've got it all, so you've got it made.'

Roger Pett gives some hints on how he writes commercials

Now read Roger Pett's advice on how to write an effective commercial before working through the Activities on page 100.

Writing commercials

As a general rule, advertising is preaching to people who aren't really interested. You may be in love with your product; eat it; sleep it; dream about it; or draw your very breath on behalf of it. But, sadly, most of the people who will be reading your ad – your potential customers – will not be quite so devoted. In fact, they probably couldn't care less. So, when you speak to them, you have to attract their attention and hold their interest.

So newspaper ads, for instance, should be designed to be at least as interesting as the news items that they sit beside. Sadly, this is not often the case.

Here is a real example from a national daily:

'Our highly advanced quality control systems ensure the strictest standards of all working procedures and components, and that the finished product conforms with this company's long held reputation for quality and value.'

A decent copywriter might have said this:

'Every one of our products is worked upon until it's perfect. If you buy it – it is.'

In other words, we take this long-winded nonsense and turn it into an easy-to-understand statement that promises the potential customer something of value – a perfect product. That is what writing effective copy is about. Making a memorable impact on people who didn't think they were interested.

How to write an effective advertisement

Each ad must say to each reader, 'Buy this product and you will get this specific benefit'.

This benefit must be one that competitors either do not or cannot offer. It must be unique in some way. The benefit must be so strong that it can attract new customers to the product.

Basic types of radio commercials

1 *The straight message*
Usually a single voice delivered in a friendly but professional manner. Ideal for business to business subjects – training services for instance, or consumer advertising for insurance, banking and that sort of thing.

2 The sketch

Frankly, these are done too often – and usually not very well. They take skill to write and are difficult to deliver unless the producers use professional actors, which 99% of the time they do not. Sadly, these seem to be the stock in trade of many radio stations who produce ads at 'no cost' as part of an air-time package. They tend to use a small range of standard situations and adapt to suit.

To these two basic formats can be added sound effects or music as required.

When I write a script I have to keep the following points in mind:

- Timing – the script for a 30 second ad should last for about 25 seconds. This allows time for music, effects, etc., and, most importantly, the clear, unhurried delivery of the message.

- When I write a script I always read it out loud and time it to the second. You cannot do this in your head, you have to deliver the script as you hope it will be delivered on air. Only this way will you get the timing right.

- I never try to imitate the style of well known personalities – the Two Ronnies for instance. Writers who do this are saying, 'Look, I don't have any ideas of my own.'

- I never use bad or suspect language, nor do I use innuendo. It is easy to offend people without even trying – so why try?

- Most importantly, remember that you have only a few seconds to make your point. Say just one thing and say it clearly. It is much better to say, 'Come to Blogg's sale for the biggest savings in town', than to try and list every item in the shop.

- The point of the ad – the main selling point – should be right up front. In other words, it should appear within the first few seconds. The listener is probably not listening anyway, and if they are they are only waiting for the next record, or the news – or something. The script must gain their immediate attention or it will fail in its main aim – to sell the product.

I hope that you will find these notes useful.

Roger Pett and Associates

innuendo – indirect reference to something insulting or rude

99

Activities

1 Which of the two Vista Vacations commercials do you prefer? Why? What makes it more successful than the other example?

2 Roger Pett describes two basic formats of radio advertisement – the straight message and the sketch. The two Vista Vacations' samples use the straight message approach: a voice simply tells us about the product.

Working on your own or in pairs, create a sketch for Vista Vacations. It could be two people on holiday, talking; people bored at home wishing they were on holiday; it could be someone listening to the weather forecast at home who decides to follow the sun; or someone who feels that their regular holiday destination has lost its excitement.

Be as creative as you can – use the possibilities of radio to catch people's imagination, with voices and sound effects creating the setting and characters. Remember to finish your advertisement with a slogan or message making it clear what makes a Vista Vacations holiday so special.

ASSIGNMENTS

1 Advertisement analysis

Study some advertisements from radio, television or print media. Choose the three most interesting examples from one of the media. If they are from television or radio, record them and transcribe them (copy out the words as a script). Then write a comparison of the three advertisements using these headings:

- what the advertisements tell us about the product
  (its main selling point; its qualities, price, etc.)

- who the advertisements seem to be aimed at
  (young, older or general audience? How can you tell? Do they seem to be aimed at women more than men?)

- the style of the advertisements
  (direct, serious, humorous, emotional, poetic?)

- which one you think is most successful and why (try to be as precise as you can in saying why you think it works well).

2 Charity advertising

Charity advertisements in newspapers and magazines can have a powerful effect upon us. Look again at the two advertisements on pages 94–95. These adverts create their impact by combining words and pictures. How would you make them work on radio?

Choose one of the advertisements and use it as the basis for a 30-second radio commercial. Your aim is to increase listeners' awareness of the charity and try to raise financial contributions. You will need to decide:

- what tone to use – serious or humorous

- what sound effects you will use

- the format – a dialogue between two people or a single voice talking directly to listeners.

ASSIGNMENTS

3 Marketing campaign

Imagine that your headteacher is keen to attract another 100 students to your school and has decided to use advertising to achieve this. Working in pairs or in small groups, create a marketing campaign. You could use:

- leaflets
- posters
- a radio commercial
- advertisements in a newspaper or magazine.

Choose one or two of these formats that you think would be most effective. Think about the unique selling points of your school – what it offers that is special and individual. Brainstorm ideas. Think of a slogan or message. Think of a range of different ideas before narrowing them down to one or two ideas to develop into finished examples.

Then present your marketing ideas to another group, or others in the class. You could make it a competition, with each group presenting its ideas to the headteacher and getting feedback on which campaign would be selected.

4 The advertising debate

Some people feel that advertising can sometimes be quite harmful. Discuss some of the issues involved by using these questions as the starting point for a debate:

- If a cigarette manufacturer offered your school £100,000 a year to advertise around the school site, should you agree?
  What if it was an alcohol company?
  Or a soft drinks manufacturer?

- Should schools be neutral places, so that advertising stays in the outside world, leaving students protected from the influence of campaigns?
  Or is that over-protecting students?

- What kind of advertising do you think is acceptable in schools?

After your debate, you could write up your ideas in a brief report, using the questions as the main subject for each paragraph.

The final frontier

Starting points

This unit is about outer space. It looks at the way we think about space, the 'final frontier', as Captain James T. Kirk called it. The unit includes:

- An extract from an old Ladybird guide to space written before any human landed on the moon. Just how accurate was it?

- The actual words spoken by Neil Armstrong and Mission Control as Armstrong took the first step on the moon's surface.

- A newspaper report about problems in space.

- Two scenes from one of the most popular space movies ever – *The Return of the Jedi*.

What is your attitude to space? Given the opportunity, would you like to travel into space, or set foot on another planet? Do you think we should be spending money on space programmes, or would the money be better spent on Earth? Why do people enjoy watching films and television shows set in space?

In a small group, discuss your response to the questions above. Then explore some of the texts that follow.

Exploring space

For centuries humans have dreamed of exploring space. In the 1950s the dream suddenly became true, as rockets carrying human beings blasted off into the Earth's atmosphere … and beyond.

Since then, advancing technology has enabled us to discover more and more about the distant planets of the universe, with probes sending back incredible colour images. Suddenly space doesn't seem so far away

In 1964, just five years before the first human stepped onto the moon, Ladybird published a book about space aimed at young readers.

Look at the extracts from the Ladybird book on pages 103–104. Does the book's approach to space travel seem exciting and magical or old-fashioned and quaint?

Storybook Space-flight

Although we think of rockets and space-travel as very new, men have dreamed for centuries about flying. They longed to soar and glide with the ease and grace of the seagull and the swallow.

A Greek writer nearly two thousand years ago wrote about a ship which was caught in a water-spout and carried up to the moon. Later he described how another daring explorer made a pair of wings and set out upon a voyage to the moon from the top of Mount Olympus, the home of the old Greek gods.

For a long time after this we do not find much about journeys into space. Then the telescope was invented and men began to learn more about the sky. A famous astronomer, named Kepler, discovered the laws which control the movements of the planets and he wrote a book telling about a voyage to the moon. Kepler's hero travelled there by the simplest way of all, by magic! He knew that there was no air between the earth and the moon and could think of no other way of getting there.

In 1638 a bishop, named Francis Godwin, told of a traveller who was carried to the moon by ten wild swans, a strange flight which you can see in the picture opposite.

A French author, Jules Verne, who lived a hundred years ago, wrote a book entitled 'From the Earth to the Moon.' His voyager was fired from a great gun, but Jules Verne forgot two very important things. His traveller would have been killed by the explosion, or roasted by the heat produced as the great shell rushed through the air.

4

The flight of the wild swans

Target—the Moon

Let us suppose that we are aboard a rocket-ship bound for the moon. It is a journey which would take about three or four days, and as our rocket roars into the sky we watch the land and sea falling behind us. The clouds, too, are soon left behind and the sky becomes a darker blue. The curve of the earth is clearly visible from a hundred miles above its surface and, after a day's journey, our planet becomes a distant globe like a big full moon. It is a water-blue colour and streaked with patches of cloud, beneath which we can see areas of green and brown where the forests and desert lands are found. At the north and south poles are the white ice-caps.

The pull of the earth's gravity is weakening and the feebler pull of the moon is growing as we approach. There is a blaze of sunshine far more intense than we find on earth, but in the shadows, when the sun is not dazzling us, the brilliant stars shine out in a sky of velvet black.

We are falling at a speed of five thousand miles an hour towards a strange world of dusty plains, rugged mountains and great craters, which has remained almost unchanged for millions of years.

Our landing is controlled by a radar set in the rocket-ship which can judge our distance accurately. At the critical moment the forward-firing jets begin to blaze. We are feeling our own weight again as the engines reduce our speed. For a few seconds there is a cloud of fire and dust and then silence. We are on the moon.

The Lunar Base

In some ways the moon is a better place for a space-station than one which is only a few hundred miles above the earth. There is no atmosphere to make the stars and planets twinkle; also the moon takes a month to turn on its axis instead of only a day. The stars would be visible for much longer and they could be seen even in the daytime. There would be no sunlight to dim their brilliance as happens in the bright blue skies we see above the earth.

Of course lunar explorers will have to eat and breathe. Oxygen must be provided to keep them alive. But not all the oxygen on the earth is found in our atmosphere. There is much in the rocks, too, although it is mixed with other things. It may exist in the rocks on the moon. Crops could be grown on the moon in specially sealed greenhouses, feeding on minerals dissolved in water. They would have fourteen days of continuous sunlight to help them grow.

Getting away from the moon would be much easier than getting away from the earth. Because of its smaller mass the moon's gravity pull is only a small fraction of that exerted by the earth.

Activities

1 Check your understanding of the Ladybird text:

1 According to the extract, why was the discovery of the telescope important?

2 How did Jules Verne imagine humans being transported into space?

3 What two problems are there with his idea?

4 Choose a sentence which you think shows the excitement of travelling to the moon.

5 Why don't the stars twinkle when seen from the moon?

Now think of three questions of your own, based on the text, to ask other people in your group.

2 Remember that the text was written in 1964, which was before humans had actually landed on the Moon's surface. Working in pairs, look for:

- clues that the text was not written recently (for example, words and phrases that seem dated; references to space-travel and exploration that no longer sound right)

- a paragraph that you really like or dislike. Say why.

3 Sometimes the text is factual and sometimes it feels more like storytelling. Try to find some examples of both styles of writing. This is one example.

Factual style	Storytelling style
A Greek writer nearly two thousand years ago wrote about a ship which was caught in a water-spout and carried up to the moon.	We are falling at a speed of five thousand miles an hour towards a strange world of dusty plains, rugged mountains and great craters ...

4 Look again at the fourth paragraph in 'Storybook Space-flight'. It describes a traveller, invented by Bishop Francis Godwin, who journeyed to the moon under the power of ten swans.

Create the opening of a story about this traveller. You could:

- write as if you were the traveller, using 'I'
- imagine the traveller as female or male
- start with her/his decision to travel to the moon, or begin with take-off
- describe the take-off as if you were someone in the watching crowd
- use the format of a diary, rather than a short story, if you prefer
- use this opening sentence:

Everyone told me my journey was impossible. Thank goodness I never once believed them. That cold Autumn evening when I set off will always stay in my mind ...

Walking on the moon

On July 20 1969, US astronaut Neil Armstrong opened the door of the Apollo II's landing craft and made history: the first human being had set foot on the moon. As Armstrong said, it was a 'giant leap for mankind'. These are the exact words he spoke during that historic moonwalk …

ARMSTRONG   I'm at the foot of the ladder. The LM foot beds are only depressed in the surface about one or two inches, although the surface appears to be very, very fine grained as you get close to it. It's almost like a powder. It's very fine. I'm going to step off the LM now.
That's one small step for man, one giant leap for mankind.
The surface is fine and powdery. I can pick it up loosely with my toe. It does adhere in fine layers like powdered charcoal to the sole and the sides of my boots. I only go in a small fraction of an inch, maybe an eighth of an inch but I can see the footprints of my boots and the treads in the fine sandy particles.
There seems to be no difficulty in moving around this and we suspect that it's even perhaps easier than the simulations of 1/6 G that we performed in various simulations on the ground. Actually no trouble to walk around. The descent engine did not leave a crater of any size. It has about one-foot clearance on the ground. We're essentially on a very level place here. I can see some evidence of rays emanating from the descent engine, but a very insignificant amount.

HOUSTON   Neil, this is Houston. Did you copy about the contingency sample? Over.

ARMSTRONG   Roger. Going to get to that just as soon as I finish these picture series.

ALDRIN   Are you going to get the contingency sample? Okay. That's good.

ARMSTRONG   It has a stark beauty all its own. It's like much of the high desert of the United States. It's different but it's very pretty out here. Be advised that a lot of the rock samples out here, the hard rock samples have what appear to be vesicles in the surface. Also, as I look at one now that appears to have some sort of feenacres.

HOUSTON   Roger. Out.

ARMSTRONG   This has been about six or eight inches into the surface. It's easy to push on it. I'm sure I could push it in farther but it's hard for me to bend down farther than that.

ALDRIN   I didn't know you could throw so far, Neil.

ARMSTRONG   See me throw things? Is my pocket open?

ALDRIN   Yes it is. It's not up against your suit, though. Hit it back once more. More toward the inside. Okay that's good.

ARMSTRONG   Put it in the pocket.

ALDRIN   Yes. Push down. Got it? No it's not all the way in. Push. There you go.

ARMSTRONG   The sample is in the pocket. My oxygen is 81 per cent. I have no flags and I'm in minimum flow.

HOUSTON   Roger, Neil.

ALDRIN   How far are my feet from the …?

ARMSTRONG   Okay, you're right at the edge of the porch.

ALDRIN   Now I want to back up and partially close the hatch - making sure not to lock it on my way out.

ARMSTRONG   ... Good thought.

ALDRIN   That's our home for the next couple of hours; we want to take good care of it. Okay, I'm on the top step and I can look down over the LCU and landing-gear pad. It's a very simple matter to hop down from one step to the next.

ARMSTRONG   Yes, I found that to be very comfortable, and walking is also very comfortable, Houston.

ARMSTRONG   You've got three more steps and then a long one.

ALDRIN   Okay. I'm going to leave that one foot up there and both hands down to about the fourth rung up.

ARMSTRONG   Now I think I'll do the same.
A little more. About another inch. There you got it. That's a good step.
About a three footer.
Beautiful view.
Ain't that somethin'?

LM – lunar module: the landing craft which carried Neil Armstrong to the moon's surface from the orbiting Apollo rocket

foot beds – the flat shapes at the base of the lunar module's four legs

simulations of 1/6 G – the astronauts practised on earth with reduced gravity

emanating – coming from

contingency sample – some moon-rocks which will be brought to Earth for analysis

vesicles – blisters

Activities

1 Working in a group of three, read aloud the text about walking on the moon, trying to make it sound as real as possible. Each of you should play one of the three voices:

Armstrong —the astronaut who is setting foot on the moon s surface

Aldrin —the astronaut who follows Armstrong from the lunar module onto the moon

Houston —the voice at NASA, space control centre in Texas.

Spend some time practising because the text contains a number of technical terms. Then record it onto cassette, perhaps adding crackling microphone noises (or any other sound effects you can think of) to make it sound more realistic.

2 Test your understanding of the text. Finish these sentences with information from the text:

1 The surface of the moon is _____.

2 Its texture is _____.

3 When you walk on it _____.

4 The surface of the moon reminds Neil Armstrong of _____.

5 Overall, the main impression of the moon s surface is that _____.

3 What must it have been like to be the first human to set foot on the moon? For centuries people had thought about visiting distant planets, but few thought it would ever be possible. Suddenly, a frontier has been reached. In pairs make up an interview with Neil Armstrong, in which you ask him about:

● what the moon was like

● what walking on the moon was like

● what he meant when he said beautiful view

● how he felt as he stepped out of the lunar module

● how the experience might have changed his life.

One of you play the interviewer, the other Neil Armstrong.

Too short for space

The following newspaper article, from the on-line *Independent* (the Internet edition of the newspaper), describes a more recent space story. Look in particular at the way the writer describes the events. Is she being neutral in her reporting, or does she seem to be slightly poking fun, even sneering, at the subject?

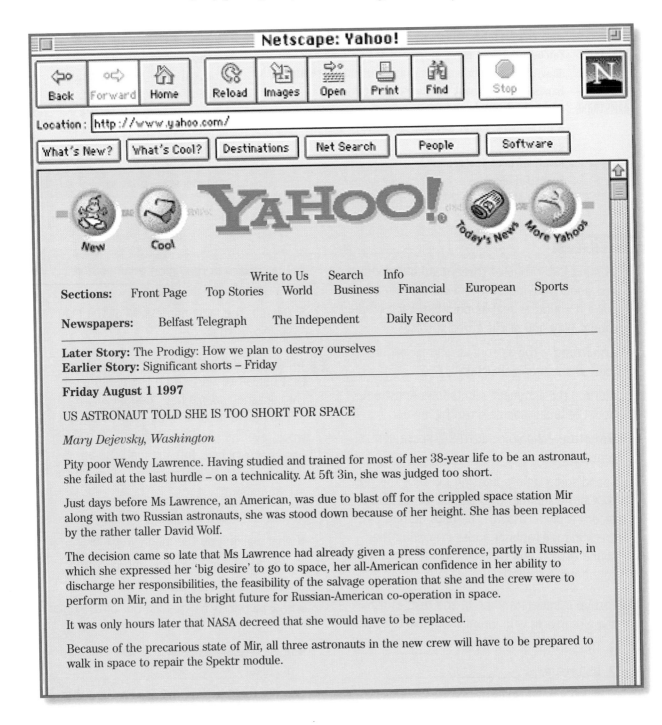

Netscape: Yahoo!

Back Forward Home   Reload Images Open Print Find   Stop

Location: http://www.yahoo.com/

What's New?   What's Cool?   Destinations   Net Search   People   Software

New   Cool   YAHOO!   Today's News   More Yahoos

Write to Us   Search   Info

Sections: Front Page   Top Stories   World   Business   Financial   European   Sports

Newspapers: Belfast Telegraph   The Independent   Daily Record

Later Story: The Prodigy: How we plan to destroy ourselves
Earlier Story: Significant shorts – Friday

Friday August 1 1997

US ASTRONAUT TOLD SHE IS TOO SHORT FOR SPACE

Mary Dejevsky, Washington

Pity poor Wendy Lawrence. Having studied and trained for most of her 38-year life to be an astronaut, she failed at the last hurdle – on a technicality. At 5ft 3in, she was judged too short.

Just days before Ms Lawrence, an American, was due to blast off for the crippled space station Mir along with two Russian astronauts, she was stood down because of her height. She has been replaced by the rather taller David Wolf.

The decision came so late that Ms Lawrence had already given a press conference, partly in Russian, in which she expressed her 'big desire' to go to space, her all-American confidence in her ability to discharge her responsibilities, the feasibility of the salvage operation that she and the crew were to perform on Mir, and in the bright future for Russian-American co-operation in space.

It was only hours later that NASA decreed that she would have to be replaced.

Because of the precarious state of Mir, all three astronauts in the new crew will have to be prepared to walk in space to repair the Spektr module.

Usually only two of the three crew members need to be equipped for space-walking. Mir was built by the Russians, to Russian specifications, and anyone who steps or floats outside has to wear a Russian 'Orlan' spacesuit that will connect with the Mir technology.

Unfortunately for Ms Lawrence, Russian spacesuits come in a one-size-fits-all (Russians). She would have been floating inside the suit before she even stepped outside. So she had to cede her place.

That, at least, is the story told by the Americans. They said it was a Russian decision; but the Russians seemed confused last night, and claimed they hadn't been told. There was a lingering suspicion that Ms Lawrence was stood down from a prospectively dangerous journey for some other reason.

Ms Lawrence has had bad luck with Mir. She was initially rejected for the programme and, at her press conference, she managed to knock the model of Mir off the table – not the best omen.

Search   News   Help

Later Story: The Prodigy: How we plan to destroy ourselves
Earlier Story: Significant Shorts – Friday
Sections: Front Page   Top Stories   World   Business   Financial   European   Sports

Newspapers: Belfast Telegraph   The Independent   Daily Record

sneering – talking or writing in an unpleasant scornful way
discharge her responsibilities – do the job
feasibility – possible success
decreed – ordered
cede – give up
prospectively – possibly
omen – sign of a future event

Activities

1 What is the official reason that Wendy Lawrence is no longer being sent into space? The writer says that there is 'a lingering suspicion that Ms Lawrence was stood down ... for some other reason ...'. Discuss what you understand by this.

2 Look more closely at the way the writer describes Wendy Lawrence. Do you think she writes fairly about her? Look in particular at her use of these words and phrases:

- 'Pity poor Wendy Lawrence'
- 'her all-American confidence'
- 'at her press conference, she managed to knock the model of Mir off the table ...'.

3 Imagine you are Wendy Lawrence. You are deeply disappointed at not being allowed to go into space, and you dislike the way this article portrays you. Write a letter to the newspaper expressing your feelings. You might mention:

- the time you had spent training
- the seriousness of your mission
- how you feel the article trivialises and pokes fun at you and your mission
- some of the words and phrases you dislike
- how the article could have been improved.

109

Battle in space

The films in the *Star Wars* series have been hugely popular. The following extract is taken from the screenplay of the third movie, *Return of the Jedi*. The forces of darkness, led by the evil Darth Vader, are about to do battle with Han Solo, Luke and Princess Leia, who are on board a stolen shuttle …

Int. – interior scene	
Ext. – exterior scene	

INT. EMPEROR'S THRONE ROOM

The converted control room is dimly lit, except for a pool of light at the far end. There the EMPEROR *sits in an elaborate control chair before a large window which looks out across the half-completed Death Star to the giant green Moon of Endor.*

DARTH VADER, *standing with the other members of the Imperial Council, cautiously approaches his Master. The ruler's back is to* VADER. *After several tense moments, the* EMPEROR'S *chair rotates around to face him.*

VADER What is thy bidding, my Master?

EMPEROR Send the fleet to the far side of Endor. There it will stay until called for.

VADER What of the reports of the Rebel fleet massing near Sullust?

EMPEROR It is of no concern. Soon the Rebellion will be crushed and young Skywalker will be one of us! Your work here is finished, my friend. Go out to the command ship and await my orders.

VADER Yes, my Master.

VADER *bows, then turns and exits the throne room as the* EMPEROR *walks towards the waiting council members.*

EXT. SPACE – DEATH STAR – MOON

There is a great deal of Imperial traffic in the area as construction proceeds on the Death Star. Transports, TIE fighters, and a few Star Destroyers move about. Now the huge Super Star Destroyer announces itself with a low roar and soon fills the frame.

INT. STOLEN IMPERIAL SHUTTLE – COCKPIT

HAN *looks back at* LUKE *and* LEIA *as* CHEWIE *flips several switches. Through the viewscreen, the Death Star and the huge Super Star Destroyer can be seen.*

HAN If they don't go for this, we're gonna have to get outta here pretty quick, Chewie.

CHEWIE *growls his agreement.*

CONTROLLER (*over radio*) We have you on our screen now. Please identify.

HAN Shuttle Tydirium requesting deactivation of the deflector shield.

CONTROLLER (*over radio*) Shuttle Tydirium, transmit the clearance code for shield passage.

HAN Transmission commencing.

LEIA *and* CHEWBACCA *listen tensely as the sound of a highspeed transmission begins.*

LEIA Now we find out if that code is worth the price we paid.

HAN It'll work. It'll work.

CHEWIE *whines nervously.* LUKE *stares at the huge Super Star Destroyer that looms ever larger before them.*

LUKE Vader's on that ship.

HAN Now don't get jittery, Luke. There are a lot of command ships. Keep your distance though, Chewie, but don't look like you're trying to keep your distance.

CHEWIE *barks a question.*

HAN I don't know. Fly casual.

LUKE I'm endangering the mission. I shouldn't have come.

HAN It's your imagination, kid. Come on. Let's keep a little optimism here.

CHEWIE *barks his worries as the Super Star Destroyer grows larger out of the window.*

INT. VADER'S STAR DESTROYER – BRIDGE

LORD VADER stands, back to us, staring out of a window at the Death Star. Now, some vibration felt only by him causes him to turn. After a moment of stillness, he walks down the row of controllers to where ADMIRAL PIETT is leaning over the tracking screen of the CONTROLLER we've seen earlier. PIETT straightens at VADER's approach.

VADER   Where is that shuttle going?

PIETT   *(into comlink)* Shuttle Tydirium, what is your cargo and destination?

PILOT VOICE   *(filtered)* Parts and technical crew for the forest moon.
(HAN)

The BRIDGE COMMANDER looks to VADER for a reaction.

VADER   Do they have a code clearance?

PIETT   It's an older code, sir, but it checks out. I was about to clear them.

VADER looks upward, as he senses LUKE's presence.

PIETT   Shall I hold them?

VADER   No. Leave them to me. I will deal with them myself.

PIETT   *(surprised)* As you wish, My Lord. *(to CONTROLLER)* Carry on.

PIETT nods at the CONTROLLER, who switches on his comlink.

INT. STOLEN IMPERIAL SHUTTLE – COCKPIT

The group waits tensely.

HAN   They're not goin' for it, Chewie.

CONTROLLER   *(filtered)* Shuttle Tydirium, deactivation of the shield will commence immediately. Follow your present course.

Everyone breathes a sigh of relief. Everyone but LUKE, who looks worried. CHEWIE barks.

HAN   Okay! I told you it was gonna work. No problem.

EXT. SPACE – STOLEN IMPERIAL SHUTTLE – ENDOR

The stolen Imperial shuttle moves off towards the green Sanctuary Moon.

EXT. FOREST LANDING SITE – ENDOR

The stolen Imperial shuttle sits in a clearing of the moon's dark primeval forest, dwarfed by the ancient, towering trees.

On an adjacent hill, the helmeted Rebel contingent makes its way up a steep trail. LEIA and HAN are slightly ahead of CHEWIE and LUKE. The troops of the strike-team squad follow, with ARTOO and THREEPIO bringing up the rear. ARTOO beeps.

Up ahead, CHEWIE *and* LEIA *reach a crest in the hill and drop suddenly to the ground, signalling the rest of the group to stop.* HAN *and* LUKE *crawl up to take a look.*

THREEPIO   Oh, I told you it was dangerous here.

Their POV: not far below them, two IMPERIAL SCOUTS *are wandering through bushes in the valley below. Their two rocket bikes are parked nearby.*

LEIA   Shall we try and go around?

HAN   It'll take time. The whole party'll be for nothing if they see us.

LEIA *motions for the squad to stay put, then she,* HAN, LUKE, *and* CHEWIE *start quietly down.*

EXT. FOREST CLEARING – CAMPSITE

The four friends make their way to the edge of the clearing not far from the two IMPERIAL SCOUTS.

HAN   Chewie and I will take care of this. You stay here.

LUKE   Quietly, there might be more of them out there.

HAN   *(grins)* Hey … it's me.

He and CHEWIE *turn and start through the bushes towards the* SCOUTS. LUKE *and* LEIA *exchange smiles.*

> **primeval** – from prehistoric times
> **contingent** – group
> **POV** – point of view

Activities

1 In groups of four or five, practise reading the screenplay aloud so that you make it as fluent and fast-moving as possible. You could record the dialogue onto cassette and listen to it, to check how smooth your reading is. You will need voices for the parts listed below. Except for the characters of Darth Vader, the Emperor and Han Solo, each reader could play several parts. Someone could also read the directions in italics.

- Darth Vader
- Emperor
- Han Solo
- Controller
- Leia
- Luke
- Piett
- Chewie
- Threepio

2 Compare the characters in the extract. Try to find some examples to show that:
- Vader is evil
- Vader is powerful
- Han is brave
- Han is calm
- Han has a positive outlook
- Han has a sense of humour
- Luke is nervous.

3 What do you think happens next? How do the different characters react to being in the forest? Try to write the next scene, using a similar layout to the screenplay used here.

ASSIGNMENTS

1 Space information

The Ladybird book about space gives young readers information about space travel and planets, and at the same time suggests the excitement of the topic. It manages to be informative *and* entertaining.

Try to do the same. Write an entry for a children's encyclopaedia about one of the topics below. Research the information, using reference books, CD-ROMs and the Internet. Then write 150 words about the topic, aiming to make it both interesting and enjoyable to read. You could:

- use a variety of short and long sentences to hold your reader's interest

- make your reader feel involved in the topic by using some storytelling techniques (for example 'As you climb aboard the space shuttle, you pause and turn to wave at the cameras. Millions of eyes are watching you as you say farewell to Earth …')

- keep your paragraphs short, so that your text seems to move quickly

- use lively, dramatic language ('the dark depths of space', 'the explosive roar of the rockets').

Topics

Choose one of these topics:

- the planets Mars, Saturn or Jupiter (choose one)

- a brief history of the space shuttle

- astronomy (star-watching).

2 Movie pitch

Before any film is begun, the makers create a 'pitch'. This is an outline of what the film will be about, who will star in it, and why they think it will be a hit. They present their pitch to the producers at the film studios, who then decide whether to give the film the go-ahead.

Here's your chance to create a film from scratch. Think of a storyline for a film set in space. Think what happens and who the main characters are. Choose actors who would be good in the roles. Think about who the film would appeal to.

You could make this assignment into a whole-class competition. Choose a group of three to play producers. This group discusses what they will be looking for in a project and how they will decide which project to support. In pairs, or in small groups, the rest of the class creates a presentation for the producers. Put together a three-minute description of your project which will make the producers want to back your film. Each group then makes their presentation. Finally, the producers choose which project they will support and explain why.

Hints

- In your presentation, don't rely too much on reading a script, or even notes – if you read, it will be harder to sound enthusiastic about your film. Try to look at the producers as you speak, rather than at a page of writing.

- Divide the roles. One of you could give the introduction to the topic – the film title and who it is aimed at; another could describe the storyline; another could talk about the characters and casting of actors.

- You could use a handout or OHP slide to make your presentation seem more formal and professional.

Day in the life

Starting points

This unit looks at people's lives – people from the past and people from other societies. It contains texts which are autobiographies, letters, and articles. Together, they give us a glimpse into the thoughts and feelings of other people.

What is your life like? If you could live in a different time-period, or in a different country, when and where would you choose? Why? What kind of life would you live there – fast-paced, glamorous, simple, wealthy … ? Discuss the kinds of lifestyle which appeal to you.

Killing a kookaburra

The following extract is a piece of autobiographical writing. It describes the events of a day which haunts the author, Oodgeroo Noonuccal, for years. Her brother kills a kookaburra – a beautiful Australian kingfisher with bright markings and a special laughing cry. The children are horrified at what they have done …

One day we five older children, two boys and three girls, decided to follow the noise of the blueys and greenies screeching from the flowering gums. We armed ourselves with our slingshots and made our way towards the trees.

5 My sisters and I always shot at our quarry from the ground. The boys would climb onto the branches of the gum-trees, stand quite still, and pick out the choicest and healthiest birds in the flock. My elder brother was by far the best shot of all of us. He was always boasting about it, too. But never in front of our mother and father, because he would have been

10 punished for his vanity. He only boasted in front of us, knowing that we wouldn't complain about him to our parents.

The boys ordered us to take up our positions under the trees as quietly as possible. 'Don't make so much noise!' they told us. In spite of the disgust we felt for our boastful brother, we always let him start the shoot-

15 ing. He was a dead shot, and we all knew it. Now we watched as he drew a bead on the large bluey straight across from him. The bird seemed intent on its honey-gathering from the gum-tree. We held our breath and our brother fired.

> **blueys and greenies** – brightly-coloured birds
> **quarry** – target
> **drew a bead on** – took aim at

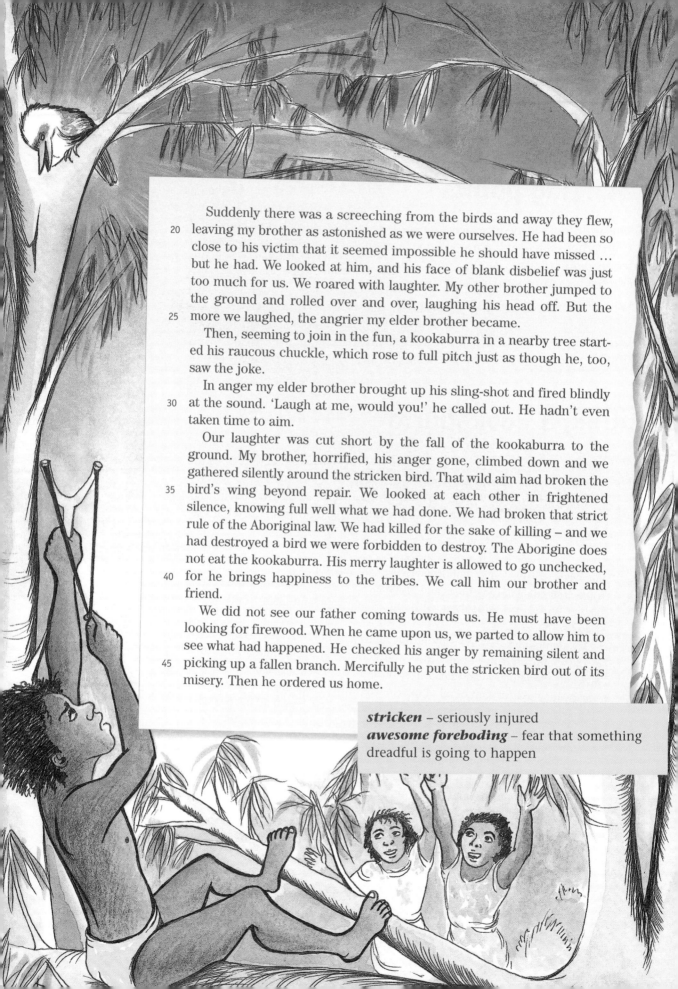

Suddenly there was a screeching from the birds and away they flew,
20 leaving my brother as astonished as we were ourselves. He had been so
close to his victim that it seemed impossible he should have missed …
but he had. We looked at him, and his face of blank disbelief was just
too much for us. We roared with laughter. My other brother jumped to
the ground and rolled over and over, laughing his head off. But the
25 more we laughed, the angrier my elder brother became.

Then, seeming to join in the fun, a kookaburra in a nearby tree started his raucous chuckle, which rose to full pitch just as though he, too,
saw the joke.

In anger my elder brother brought up his sling-shot and fired blindly
30 at the sound. 'Laugh at me, would you!' he called out. He hadn't even
taken time to aim.

Our laughter was cut short by the fall of the kookaburra to the
ground. My brother, horrified, his anger gone, climbed down and we
gathered silently around the stricken bird. That wild aim had broken the
35 bird's wing beyond repair. We looked at each other in frightened
silence, knowing full well what we had done. We had broken that strict
rule of the Aboriginal law. We had killed for the sake of killing – and we
had destroyed a bird we were forbidden to destroy. The Aborigine does
not eat the kookaburra. His merry laughter is allowed to go unchecked,
40 for he brings happiness to the tribes. We call him our brother and
friend.

We did not see our father coming towards us. He must have been
looking for firewood. When he came upon us, we parted to allow him to
see what had happened. He checked his anger by remaining silent and
45 picking up a fallen branch. Mercifully he put the stricken bird out of its
misery. Then he ordered us home.

stricken – seriously injured
awesome foreboding – fear that something
dreadful is going to happen

On the way back we talked with awesome foreboding of the punishment we knew would come. I wished our father would beat us, but we all knew it would not be a quick punishment. Besides, Dad never beat
50 us. No, we knew the punishment would be carefully weighed to fit the crime. When we got home, our mother was told to give us our meal. Nothing was said of the dead kookaburra, but we knew Dad would broach the subject after we had eaten. None of us felt hungry, and our mother only played with her food. We knew that Dad had decided upon
55 the punishment, and that Mother had agreed to it, even if she felt unhappy about it.

It was our mother who ordered us to bring into the backyard our bandicoot traps, our sling-shots, and every other weapon we had. We had to place them in a heap in the yard, while our father carefully checked every item.
60 Our big black dog stood with us. He always did that when there was trouble in the family. Although he could not possibly understand the ways of human beings, he could nevertheless interpret an atmosphere of trouble when it came.

Father spoke for the first time since we had killed the kookaburra. He
65 asked for no excuses for what we had done, and we did not offer any. We must all take the blame. That is the way of the Aborigine. Since we had killed for the sake of killing, the punishment was that for three months we should not hunt or use our weapons. For three months we would eat only the white man's hated rations.
70 During those three months our stomachs growled, and our puzzled dog would question with his eyes and wagging tail why we sat around wasting our time when there was hunting to be done.

It happened a long time ago. Yet in my dreams, the sad, suffering eyes of the kookaburra, our brother and friend, still haunt me.

Oodgeroo Noonuccal, *Killing a Kookaburra*

Activities

1 Look more closely at the setting and characters of the text. What do you learn about where the events happened, and what the girl who describes them is like? Skim-read the story, making notes like this:

Clues about the setting	Clues about the narrator's character

2 Look at the children's punishment for what they have done. They have to give up their weapons for three months, stop hunting, and only eat the white man's rations. If the events had taken place in our culture, and you were the mother or father of the children, what punishment would you have given them?

3 The extract describes a memorable event. It is written in a clear, direct way, making it easy to imagine. Now rewrite it as a script for a radio play. How would you tell the story without describing the scene in such detail? You will need to make up dialogue to show what is happening.
You could use these characters:

● the narrator (as an older person looking back)

● the narrator (as a girl)

● two sisters and two brothers

● mother and father.

You could start:

OLDER NARRATOR That day will always haunt me ...

At home in Egypt

The novelist and short story writer Penelope Lively was brought up in Egypt. This extract from her autobiography describes what her home and life were like.

I am lying on a sofa, knees hugged to my chest, staring at the sofa back, which is a blurry chintz patterned with flowers, large blue and green pansies. I have a pain in my stomach. I trace the petals of the pansies with my finger. The pain comes in great waves, ebbing and flowing,
5 washing through me as though I were in the grip of some tide. Lucy is somewhere in the room, knitting. I can hear the clack of needles. There is just the blurred pansies, and the clicking noise, and the pain.

The mosquito net over my bed is suspended from the ceiling by a metal hoop, and tucked in under the mattress all around. I am inside a filmy
10 white tent. The tent is filled with the metallic smell of Flit. I can see the outline of the Flit-gun on the table beside the bed, a chunky barrel with a pump handle. I can see also the grey smudges of squashed mosquitoes on the net and a long wavering white line where Lucy has mended a tear.

I have found a praying mantis in the hedge. A shaft of sunlight makes it
15 translucent. I can see its insides, and the dark veining of its wings, and the globes of its eyes. It sits in a frozen posture, and then moves an arm, stiffly, like an automaton.

… My bed, and the mosquito net, were in the night nursery. Lucy slept there too. Across the passage was the day nursery, in which we lived. The
20 passage reached from one end of the house to the other, and rooms opened off it to either side, like a hotel corridor – a peculiar arrangement for domestic architecture, but then it was an unusual house, or at least unlike anything I have known since. Externally, it was cream stucco with green shutters, flat-roofed and with a wide covered veranda running
25 round most of two sides. The front door was rather grandly porticoed, with a flight of steps leading up. Now, it seems to me like a small version of one of those plantation mansions of the American deep south. It had been built in the early years of the century, along with its two neigh-bours, each of them lavishly surrounded by gardens and sharing an
30 access driveway screened by a high hedge.

At the far end of that long corridor upstairs was our bathroom, which was also the visitors' bathroom, and outside its window was a palm tree in which lived an owl, which would bob up and down in a strange private gymnastic performance. This was the Egyptian Little Owl, I had been
35 told, and I always thought of it thus, with precision (heralding maybe an adult enthusiasm for extremely amateur ornithology). Next to the bathroom was Lucy's pantry, in which she had a primus stove and did small-scale cooking operations in areas over which she did not trust the kitchen servants, such as boiling the milk. On one legendary occasion
40 one of the bottles of milk delivered daily had been found to contain a small live fish – indicating that whoever bottled or delivered it was in the habit of topping it up from the canal.

Next to the pantry was our bedroom, and then the spare bedroom, and opposite was the big nursery, with the flowered chintz sofa on which I
45 languished when ailing. The nursery opened on to a veranda – the roof of the covered veranda around the ground floor. In very hot weather my parents slept on this veranda in a sort of large fruit cage. I never got to do this, and it was a focal point of dissatisfaction. Why not? Why them and not me? Strictly speaking, it was not even their territory, which was the big suite of bedroom, dressing-room and bathroom at the far end of the
50 corridor into which I seldom penetrated. Occasionally I was allowed in to explore the contents of my mother's jewellery box or to watch her apply her make-up. I perceived their quarters as qualitatively different from ours, more richly furnished and full of lavish smells (my mother's scent, my father's leather shoes) but I always felt a touch displaced there
55 and was quite happy to retreat again. Next to the nursery was a further guest bedroom, a sliver of a room reserved for bachelors, of which there was a plentiful supply, an unending stream of Eighth Army buccaneers on leave from the Western Desert. My parents were extremely gregarious; there was always someone staying, lunch parties and tea parties and
60 'people for drinks' were the norm.

chintz – light cotton fabric	**ornithology** – bird-watching
Flit – insect repellent	**primus stove** – small portable
praying mantis – large insect like a cockroach	cooker, powered using petrol or oil
	languished – lay
translucent – almost see-through	**veranda** – open terrace
porticoed – under a covered entrance supported by columns	**displaced** – not at home
	gregarious – enjoying the company of others

The front door opened on to a large hall dominated at one end by a fireplace in which a fire was lit at Christmas, for ceremonial purposes. There was a Knole settee from which I was banned because I might bounce on it or dirty the cover: I cannot set eyes on a Knole settee, to
65 this day, without a feeling of truculence, the submerged resentment of the *hoi polloi*. There was also an early nineteenth-century tallboy with brass handles in which were kept objects of importance: my father's papers, photograph albums. I was forbidden, equally, to open these drawers. The tallboy had a definite aura: it signified official, adult con-
70 cerns. Today, that tallboy stands in my bedroom in London. It houses some of my clothes, and a fair amount of detritus like surplus Christmas wrapping paper and discarded spectacles. This seems to me a nice instance of the way in which a portentous inanimate object eventually gets its come-uppance, though in another sense I still have a respect for
75 the tallboy – it has twice navigated the Mediterranean, it has an impenetrable past going back at least a hundred years before I first knew it, and it is all set to outlast me, for sure.

Penelope Lively, *Oleander Jacaranda: A Childhood Perceived*

truculence – defiant aggressiveness
hoi polloi – the masses
detritus – discarded bits and pieces

portentous – of great (often menacing) significance

Activities

1 Penelope Lively describes the interior of her home in great detail. What impression do you have of her and her family:

- their lifestyle
- their wealth
- their belongings
- their social life?

2 The house is described in considerable detail. Working either on your own or in pairs, draw a map showing the different rooms. Label the map. Compare your finished map with one produced by someone else. Did you get the details right?

3 Write a guided tour of your house or flat. Imagine you are giving someone instructions on how to find their way from the front door to your bedroom. Describe the route they will take, and what they will see on the way. Write in as much detail as possible.

Skipping school

Frank Unwin went to a school near Liverpool
during the First World War (1914–1918).
It was not a happy time as you will see
from the following biographical extract …

Dealing with a truant

I hated school so I would sag off, go down the market and do odd
jobs there. Well, when I was ten I sagged off for three weeks, and
the attendance officer he chased me across the market and got
hold of me, and the result was I was sent to this industrial school
5 for six months. They made you feel like a prisoner, like you'd
committed some great crime. You had to march everywhere;
march to your dormitory, march into meals. And most of the
time you weren't allowed to speak; you had to be silent prac
tically all day – it was to break your will. Well, I couldn't stand
10 that, because you couldn't stop me talking, so one day we had a
games lesson in a field by the sand dunes and I decided to run
away. They had boys and masters posted as sentries all round
the field, but there was lots of long grass and I managed to crawl
away without being seen. Then I ran all the way down the dunes
15 back to Liverpool, and I lived rough in the docks for a few days.
'Course, I got hungry and I decided to come back so I marched
back into the school. I was taken into the gym and the whole
school was assembled.

sag off – play truant
dormitory – sleeping quarters

> 20 They laid me out on a table and there was a boy at each corner holding down my arms and legs. Then the headmaster beat me as hard as he could. I know I was biting my collar; I had it in my mouth so that I wouldn't show any pain. I wasn't going to cry, and he hit me all the harder because I didn't. And after that I was sentenced to another four years' stay at the school as a pun-
> 25 ishment. In the end I was there longer than anybody else.

Frank Unwin, from *A Century of Childhood*

Activities

1 Look at the description Frank Unwin gives of the industrial school. What is it like? How is it different from your own school? Make a list of points using a table like the one below.

What the school is like	Differences from my school

2 Frank Unwin is treated very brutally at the school. Imagine you were his father or mother and he told you of the beating he had received. How would you react?

Either: write the conversation between you and Frank. You could start like this:

FRANK: Hello, Mum, I'm home.
YOU: Hello – look at the state of you. You're covered in marks. What's been happening?

Or: write a letter of complaint to the headmaster of the school complaining about the vicious treatment of your son. You could start:

Dear Mr Foley,

I am writing to complain about the condition my son arrived home in this evening ...

Two letters from the past

Letters often show us into the everyday lives of other people, sometimes in other cultures or other periods. Read the following two letters written by women in the early twentieth and mid-nineteenth centuries. What picture of their lives are we given?

Marina Tsvetayeva was a Russian poet. Here, in 1919, she writes to her sister Anastasia about her hard lifestyle …

Letter 1

I live with Alya and Irina (Alya is six, Irina two) in our same flat opposite two trees in the attic room which used to be Seryozha's. We have no flour and no bread. Under my writing desk there are about twelve pounds of potatoes
5 which is all that is left from the food 'lent' by my neighbours. These are the only provisions we have. I walk all over Moscow looking for bread. If Alya comes with me, I have to tie Irina to a chair, for safety. I feed Irina, then put her to bed. She sleeps in the blue armchair. There is a
10 bed but it won't go through the door. I boil up some old coffee, and drink it, and have a smoke. I write. Alya writes or reads. There is silence for two hours; then Irina wakes up. We heat up what remains of the mashed goo. With Alya's help, I fish out the potatoes which remain, or rather have
15 become clogged in the bottom of the samovar. Either Alya or myself puts Irina back to bed. Then Alya goes to bed. At 10 pm the day is over.

Elaine Feinstein, *Marina Tsvetayeva*

The Real World

Flora Tristan, writing in 1841, describes a visit to the women's prison at Newgate, London ...

Letter 2

I confess I felt very ill at ease in this lodge. There is no fresh air or daylight; the prisoner can still hear the noise of the street outside, and beneath the door he can still see the sunlight shining in the square. What a dreadful contrast, and
5 how he regrets the loss of his liberty! But once past the lodge he hears nothing more; the atmosphere is as cold, damp and heavy as in the cellar; most of the passages are narrow, and so are the stairs leading to the upper wards.

First I was taken to see the women's wing. Over the past
10 few years several changes have been made at Newgate and now it houses only prisoners awaiting trial, not convicted prisoners; in this respect it corresponds to the Conciergerie in Paris. It is here too that most executions take place.

The governor was kind enough to accompany me over the
15 prison; he told me that thanks to the writings of philanthropists and the constant complaints of humanitarians, Newgate had undergone all the improvements of which it was capable. Mr Cox was particularly happy that prisoners were now divided into different classes, whereas formerly they had all
20 been confined together.

The internal arrangement of the prison is not very satisfactory and there is not enough space for individual cells. In each ward the beds, wooden constructions six feet long and two feet wide, are arranged in two or three tiers like berths on
25 board a ship. There is a large table in the middle with wooden benches all round it; this is where the prisoners eat, work, read and write. On close examination I found the wards very clean and well kept, but as they are dark and poorly ventilated and the floors are very uneven, their general appearance is
30 unpleasing.

Nearly all the women I saw there were of the lowest class; prostitutes, servants or country girls accused of theft. Four were on charges carrying the death penalty for crimes classified as felonies under English law. Most of them seemed
35 to be of low intelligence, but I noticed several whose tight thin lips, pointed nose, sharp chin, deep-set eyes and sly look I took as signs of exceptional depravity. I saw only one woman there who aroused my interest. She was confined with six others in a dark, damp low-ceilinged cell; when we entered they
40 all rose and made us the customary servile curtsey which had embarrassed and irritated me from the moment I set foot in the prison. One alone refrained and it was this sign of independence which attracted my attention. Picture a young woman of twenty-four, small, well-made and tastefully
45 dressed, standing with head held high to reveal a perfect profile, graceful neck. My eyes filled with tears and only the presence of the governor prevented me from going up to her and taking her hand so that she might understand my interest in her fate and so that my sympathy might calm for a few
50 moments the sufferings of her heart.

Jean Hawkes (translator), *The London Journal of Flora Tristan*

Activities

1 Look at the two environments described by the writers of these letters – the home of Marina Tsvetayeva and the prison visited by Flora Tristan. Both are appalling places. Make some notes on what both environments are like:

The home in letter 1	The prison in letter 2

Compare your choice of words with someone else in your group.

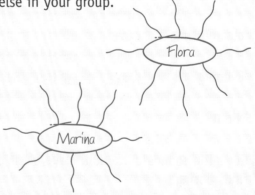

2 Look more closely at the impression we get of the two writers. Use a spider diagram for each one to describe what they seem like – cheerful, upset, angry, struggling …?

3 Imagine you are one of the women in the prison, in the second letter – perhaps the young woman of 24. How do you feel about being visited in prison? How do you feel about Flora Tristan? What does she look like? How does she look at you? What expression do you see on her face? Describe Flora's visit, from the young woman's point of view.

A life in the day of Guy the Gorilla

For many years the *Sunday Times Magazine* has run a weekly feature called 'A Life in the Day of'. It aims to show what a person is like by describing a typical day in their life. Sometimes the people are famous; sometimes they are ordinary members of the public. In 1977 one issue profiled Guy the Gorilla. Read the article on page 127 before working through the following Activities.

Activities

1 How much do we learn from the article about a typical day in the life of Guy? Look at the time chart below and fill in any details you can from the interview.

Dawn

8 am

9 am

Morning

Lunch

Afternoon

Closing time

Evening

Night

2 Guy's life sounds quite dull. Make a list of things which he finds boring.

3 Work in a group of four. Two of you think of arguments in favour of keeping animals like Guy in zoos. Two of you think of arguments against. Then have a debate about whether you believe it is fair to keep him in a cage or not.

A LIFE IN THE DAY OF GUY THE GORILLA

I always wake up at dawn but I do nothing about it. There's a very flash chimp nearby called Sidney who's always making a noise first thing, but I ignore him. They snore as well, the chimps, but not as bad as the orangs. I ignore them all. I just lie and wait for George [George Callard, head keeper of apes]. Why should I hurry?

If it's not George but some other keeper, I might give him a look, perhaps go across to the wire and try to get him, just to show who's boss. But it's usually George. I catch his eye, then I look away again, then I dart him another look. I don't go in for all this friendship stuff with human beings, not like those stupid chimps. They'll talk to everybody.

I've got three cages – my back den where I sleep, my show cage and the outside cage. Nobody's got a bigger cage. I might not be the oldest gorilla in the world – though I'm the oldest in Europe. I might not be the biggest. But I am the greatest.

Around about eight every morning I can hear them slopping around in my show cage, cleaning it out for the day. I don't know why they bother. They let me help in the old days when I was younger. I used to love the disinfectant. I drank gallons. But some rotten zoologist comes along and says it's bad for me. They keep me absolutely separate now. I used to play with Smithy, my old keeper. We had some great games, wrestling, pushing. I thought he liked being clutched a few hours at a time. I suppose I am a big fellow, about 7ft around the chest – not that anyone has ever dared measure me. It was just good fun.

At nine o'clock George opens the sliding doors and I go into my show cage for

breakfast. It's always the same old stuff – a large bowl of Cooper's pellets. Monkey chow, so George calls it. They're scattered all over the floor and I have to scratch around to pick them up. Very undignified. I get 800 grams every morning and Lomie gets 700 grams.

I hoped you wouldn't ask about Lomie. Okay, she's a lady gorilla. She has her own back den but we share the rest of the quarters. She came here in 1969, I think it was. I'd been on my own for over 20 years. They'd tried to find a mate several times but either couldn't afford the prices or they died en route. I told them I didn't care, but they went on and on about it. If you ask me, it was PR.

I spend most of the morning munching my disgusting breakfast. Lomie nicks most of it. I can't work up the energy. Gives me something to do instead of watching the stupid humans. You wouldn't believe the cretinous remarks I've had to put up with over the years. 'Look, it's King Kong.' 'Ooh, isn't he like our Dad?' The afternoons are the worst, especially on Sundays and bank holidays. It's standing room only for miles around. I deliberately sit still, doing absolutely nothing for up to an hour, just to teach them. Then, when I move, they all shriek.

There are some nice humans. Where's the postcard? Mr and Mrs Heaton, that's it. He's a retired master plumber from near Leeds. I get cards all the time, and on my birthday. They've come regular for years, spend every day of their holidays here, just to see me. Ask George.

I can remember the day it happened in 1968 – the day they banned the public from feeding the animals. I used to get through up to 20 ice-cream cartons a day, plus as many sweets as I could grab, then overnight, wham, it all stopped. I lay down in my cage for three days and moaned.

I hardly ever go out in winter. Lomie's always dashing out, jumping on the bars. But the first spot of rain, I'm right in, no messing. Not her, though. Says she loves the rain. Stupid bitch.

Closing time's the best part of the day – that's when I get the real food. Tonight, let's see, George says I'm getting six bananas, one pear, two tomatoes, half a cucumber, bunch of grapes, four apples, a slice of cabbage, a lettuce and a packet of dates. I also get two pints of milk.

I sit up to eat that awful pellet stuff in the morning, but at night I lie down on one elbow on my straw. George says I look like a Roman. If I want to get really comfy I lie flat on my stomach.

It's a pretty draggy life, being cooped up here all day. The days really are boring and I hate the crowds, but if you're the greatest you expect people to come. I don't get bothered at night, not since they put Lomie in her own cage. We don't sleep together, thank God. I eat in peace and quiet and then it's heads down, and I'm off.

Interview by
Hunter Davies
Photograph by
David Reed

cretinous – extremely stupid

ASSIGNMENTS

1 Time of regrets

Think of a time when you have done something which you realised was wrong. It might have seemed a good idea at first, but it went horribly wrong and caused damage or pain. Describe what happened in detail. Try to:

- describe when the event happened – how old you were
- describe the setting – what you remember about where it took place. Give as much detail as possible
- describe what happened – tell your story step by step
- finish by thinking about what went wrong, how you felt, and any lessons you have learnt from the experience.

2 Interview

Interview someone about their memories of childhood. You could choose a grandparent or friend of your family. Try to find out what it was like to be young then. How different was it? What did people eat? What did they do for entertainment? What were the insides of houses like? Find out as much detail as you can. Then write up your interview as an article about the person. Call it, 'The childhood days of … .'

3 Life in the Day of …

Write your own 'Life in the Day of …' article based on a typical day in your own life. You could choose a weekend or schoolday. Describe your routines and habits, people you meet, things you like and dislike. Your article should give your reader a vivid picture of what you and your typical day are like.